HOW TO BE
H.O.T.

HOW TO BE
H.O.T.

Your Guide to Becoming
HAPPY, OPEN and TRUSTING
In Your Relationships

CHRISTAL FUENTES
FOUNDER OF *The Ladies Coach*

PAGE STREET
PUBLISHING CO.

PAGE STREET
PUBLISHING CO.

First published in 2016 by
Page Street Publishing Co.
27 Congress Street, Suite 103
Salem, MA 01970
www.pagestreetpublishing.com

Distributed by Macmillan, sales in Canada by The Canadian Manda Group.

19   18   17   16   1   2   3   4   5

ISBN-13: 9781624142864
ISBN-10: 1624142869

Library of Congress Control Number: 2016934581

Cover and book design by Page Street Publishing Co.
Photography by Melinda Jae Johnson

Printed and bound in the U.S.A.

Page Street is proud to be a member of 1% for the Planet. Members donate one percent of their sales to one or more of the over 1,500 environmental and sustainability charities across the globe who participate in this program.

To the love of my life, Andrew. Thank you for always being my rock and supporting my dream in every way a person can. I'm inspired every day with your love.

Why Being HOT Matters

Happiness.

Such a beautiful yet super cliché word, isn't it? The word *happiness* gets thrown around so much that we start to lose sense of what it actually means to feel happy.

We know that being happy is a feeling we want to achieve, but the very act of "achieving" happiness turns it into an end goal. It becomes something to seek behind all the "what ifs" of life. "Happiness" turns into a game, a struggle, a competition or a future experience because happiness is a feeling that's undeserving of being felt *right now*.

Why should we have to wait for happiness? Why can't we feel deserving of being happy right now? Before we make X amount of dollars, lose X amount of weight or get that dream job with that dream position that comes with that dream house?

How can we make happiness a part of the journey instead of our end goal? Well ... that's exactly what we are going to try and figure out throughout this book because that's really why you're reading this, right?

You want to know how to be HOT in your relationships, and we're not talking about the "hot" that requires a push-up bra, red lipstick and super uncomfortable high heels to wear in order to feel sexy—although I do love all of the above (if there are flats readily available).

I'm talking about becoming Happy. Open. Trusting. Because the truth is, in all of my nearly thirty years on earth, that's where true joy and fulfillment have lived for me.

Oh yeah, maybe I should introduce who "me" is, because we are going to get pretty personal in these upcoming chapters, plus you might be wondering how I know so much about happiness. Well, the truth is ... I didn't go to college for this stuff (or at all, for that matter).

I don't have a fancy certificate or a degree in psychology, and I certainly won't claim to be an expert, as the media likes to quickly label coaches in the field these days; I will say that I have been, and always will be, a student of life and have been vigorously taking notes from some of the major lessons (breakdowns) I've gone through and still go through from time to time.

I truthfully wouldn't be where I am today (if I'm anywhere at all) without people. People who have loved me, people who saw my purest intention, people who gave their time for me, people who wanted to see me succeed, people who have hurt me, people who have betrayed me, people who didn't understand me, people who came with significant lessons, people who brought on that "tough love," people with passionate energy, people who inspired me …

Who I am today comes from the relationships I have had and the reason why I believe relationships are one of the most fundamental keys to fulfillment in life. Relationships guide and shape the soul, good or bad, and what I've come to find out and truly believe is the relationship you have with yourself sets the foundation for the relationships you have with others.

Let me say this again, and trust me, you will see this quotation of mine stamped on almost everything I do because, well … it's the truth: *The relationship you have with yourself sets the foundation for the relationships you have with others.*

And that's what we are going to talk about (most of the time) because what I have found and am still finding in my personal journey is that the deeper the connection and love I have with myself, the more quality relationships I have around me. The more distant the connection I have with myself (mixed with a little judgment), the more toxic the relationships I have around me.

Now, when I say "relationships," most people automatically assume "intimate" relationships, which is definitely a part of it and certainly one we will be talking about, but just so we are on the same page throughout this journey together, let me give you some guideposts of all the relationships that we are currently in right *now*. It might also be a good idea to take a mental note of where you might be with each one. The best way to do this is to go by the feeling you get when you see each one.

I'm a feelings type of person, and feelings don't really lie because they come from your gut. So as you read each below, I ask you: How do you feel?

- **Self:** Have to start there, right? The most important relationship *ever*! Why? Because, again, this is the foundation of all other relationships.

- **Spirituality:** Hmmm … This one is different for everyone, but it all comes from the *faith* we have for something beyond ourselves, and since we will be talking about trust later, this might come as an important one.

Being *selfish*
is the most
unselfish thing
you can be.

- **Health/Body:** Whewww! Even as I write this I felt a little judgment come through, so I'm right there with you, but here's the truth: Our body is all we've got, and it does so much for us, yet we often neglect it, tear it apart and then criticize it!

- **Personal Relationships/Family/Friends/Acquaintances/Coworkers:** Who are the people around you and how do you *feel* around them?

- **Love:** Do you have an intimate partner? Single and ready to mingle ... or not? Maybe you've been betrayed in your past and finding love a little hard to jump back into? Regardless of where you are, one thing I do believe is that intimate love is the most spiritual of practices and one that can inspire the soul the most, or, unfortunately, damage it the most.

- **Money/Professional/Job:** Dolla dolla bills, ya'll. Okay, you might now be wondering, "How is money a relationship? It's a material thing!" I know, I hear this a lot and was totally there—trust me! But the fact of the matter is, money is a form of energy (like all other relationships) that can either drain you and make you feel disempowered or enhance your life for the better.

- **Purpose/Passion/Creativity:** Huuuuuge one! What do you enjoy doing? What lights you up? What are you doing for yourself that restores the energy you already put out into the world and energizes your spirit?

Now, by taking a good look at these guideposts, which relationship(s) did you feel like, "Yeah ... I definitely need a little work on that!" and which relationship(s) do you know you absolutely rock at?

We all have areas where we are superstars and areas we'd rather not mention, and even more, sweep under the rug, right? Well, the truth is, in order for us to become HOT mamas, we have to declare what's working and what's not working. And guess what? You'll find that there's not this huge makeover you have to do with your life (cough cough, *relationships*). There just might be some little tweaks and fixes you need to do that will drastically change how you feel. And that's just what we are going to do together.

How to Use This Book

Because I love clear-cut directions myself (otherwise I'm a space cadet), I'm going to tell you the best way to use this book, but by all means, feel free to use this however you want because, either way, I know you will get something out of it.

Remember the guideposts of relationships? The relationships you currently feel are lacking in your life will be exactly what we cover throughout the book. No, I'm not a psychic and no, the book doesn't change based on what you choose, but no matter where you are in your journey, the insights and practices are pretty universal (at least in my findings).

Say Thank You

Don't turn the page just yet! First, can we start with a "thank you"?

I'd like you to say thank you to yourself. Say thank you for bringing yourself this far. Say thank you to yourself for wanting to expand your heart and mind. Say thank you for all the love you have given to others and continue to give to others. Say thank you for all that you have accomplished, large or small.

Just recently I was with my dearest mentor, whom I've seen every Sunday for the past six years. He had stopped me in the midst of my rambling one day and said, "Shhh ... can you just take the time to say thank you for all the good things you were responsible for in your life?" He continued, "Your homework this week is to do nothing but remember all the moments you should be proud about and say 'thank you.'"

I was stumped. The more I thought about it, the clearer it was that I never really appreciate what I do for myself. And that's really what I wish I could have done more of. So let's start saying thank you from this day forward. There are so many magical moments that we are responsible for, and we need to start recognizing them and be more grateful.

Now, I'm not saying we need to start a Disney parade every time we are proud of ourselves, but I am saying that acknowledging those magical moments and saying "thank you" will make us more connected to who we are. This is the key to becoming happy, open and trusting.

One

Let's Get Real!
What's Your Story?

Story time! This exploration shouldn't be hard because we've got a lot of them, don't we? You know, the stories that keep us creating disempowering beliefs about the world. What are disempowering beliefs? They are beliefs that keep us feeling shitty and stuck. Here's some to get your creative juices flowing:

"There are just no good guys (girls) out there."

"I'm not educated enough for the position I want."

"I'm too young."

"I'm too old."

"My partner will never change his (her) ways."

"This is as good as it gets."

"I'm not pretty enough, smart enough, rich enough."

"There's just not enough time."

"This is the life I was given."

"No man (woman) can keep up with me."

"I'm just too smart for people."

"I'm gonna be single the rest of my life."

"Passion is for the movies."

Take some time to think about what your disempowering beliefs are. I encourage you to think really hard, because the truth is, we all have them. We might not even know the stories we are telling ourselves until we dissect what's keeping us feeling stuck and it requires us to get real!

All of our negative beliefs, large or small, are attached to a story we've made up in our head and confused with fact. Let me give you an example of a small disempowering belief that I had to get over just recently. It had to do with writing this book, as a matter of fact. I'm probably throwing myself under the bus a bit, but that's okay.

If you didn't know, this is my first book. (Celebrate good times!) A big hooray, right?! Well, with that blessing came a lot of procrastination. There were days I planned just for writing but quickly found everything else more important. It got so bad that my man, Andrew, would often (okay, all day, every day) ask me when I was going to write. I would usually pick out one of the following three excuses. Want to hear them? I thought they were pretty good.

"After I work out, so I can get that out of the way and focus." (Five hours later.)

"There are too many people at the house causing too much distraction, so when they leave."

"I'm too tired. I had a really busy day, so I will focus on it tomorrow."

Again, these were only some of the excuses I gave on the daily. However, the real reason I was procrastinating was because I was deathly afraid. After the excitement wore off, I realized that writing a book comes with completely putting myself and my work out there, and that's scary as hell! Why was it scary? Because there was a small voice inside that said, "You're not good enough, Christal. You don't really know enough, Christal. You're not a writer, Christal. Who's going to read your book, Christal?"

I didn't really want to acknowledge these voices were what was stopping me until I sat down and got real about why I was procrastinating, and let me tell you, becoming aware was even scarier! I mean, these voices (beliefs) each had their own megaphone in my head. It was cringing, hurtful, suffocating and frightening. My spirit suffered. My message suffered. My passion suffered. And although these voices (beliefs) were primarily about writing my first book, they were backed by tons of experiences from my past. Not to mention, these voices came with energy. Energy that completely sucked the inspiration right out of me. Energy that filtered every aspect of my life, causing me to feel uncertain of who I was in general.

Remember how I said this was just a small belief I had recently? It doesn't sound that small now, given the huge impact it had on my spirit. But the truth is, so many of us are walking around with not one, not two, but hundreds of disempowering beliefs that are leaving our spirits feeling unworthy of the things we want most.

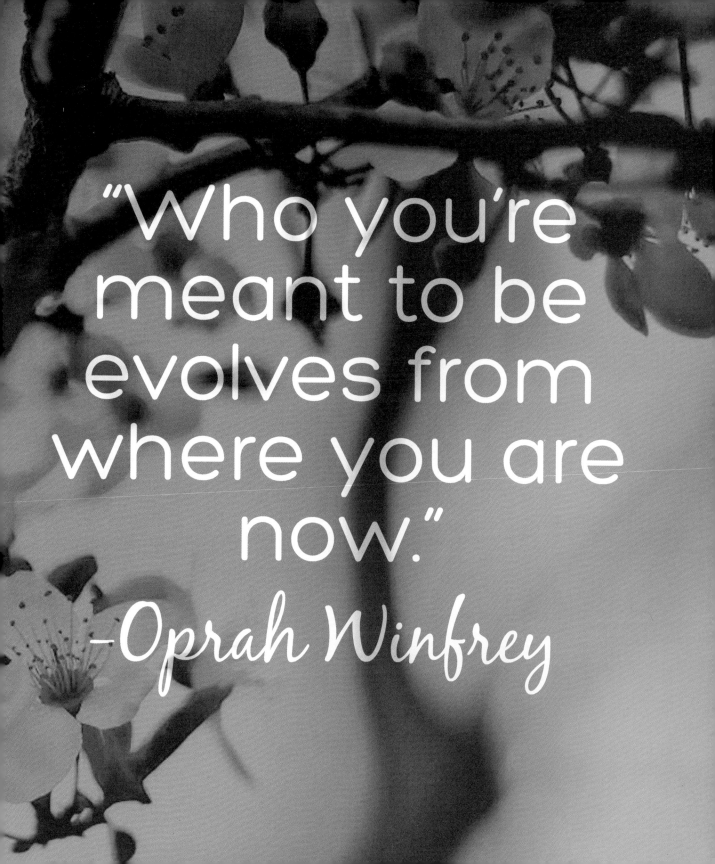

"Who you're meant to be evolves from where you are now."

-Oprah Winfrey

You can fool the world, but when you believe you can fool yourself; that's when you become a danger to yourself.

How in the hell are we supposed to feel happy when we are walking around with beliefs and stories that restrict who we are? Oh yes, let's talk about our stories! Now that I told you about my beliefs that came in the form of a troll's voice, and I'm not talking about the cute trolls with gem belly buttons that we used to play with when we were younger—I'm talking about gremlin trolls! These trolls also happen to create untrue, or fabricated, stories and disguise them as fact. You know how they do this? They will take a story from your past, twist the feelings that arise from it into a disempowering belief and then hope the resulting "belief" sticks until you actually think the voices are true!

Trolls love to manipulate stories to make what they have to say true. If I didn't go back and acknowledge these voices by getting real with what was going on, I wouldn't have been able to understand what was causing me to cave into fear. Are you starting to see how this works?

Now, I don't want you to feel overwhelmed, but I do encourage you to think of your most recent disempowering belief and acknowledge how it has made you feel. Then ask yourself, Is this really true? Or is it coming from a troll?

In order for us to become HOT in our relationships we have to stop the bullshit beliefs we have regarding them. Getting real requires you to take a step or two (or for some of us, a few more) inward to see what standards we've allowed in our life versus what we ultimately want. What we will find is there might be a contradiction between our "wants" and our "truths."

Let me repeat that again. There's usually a contradiction between our "wants" and our "truths."

The problem is less about knowing what we actually want. We usually know what we want and if we say we don't it's because we often feel embarrassed actually saying what we want. The problem is that how we are currently living is not congruent with what we ultimately want.

Raise your hand if you know someone (maybe you) who finds herself in and out of a toxic relationship and very often says, "I just want a man who treats me [this] way ... Does [this] for me ... Makes me feel like [this]" (insert your preferences as needed). We usually don't have a problem expressing what we want, but why is it so hard to get what we want?

It's because our wants don't align with our truths. Our truth is how we exist now. And how we exist now is an accumulation of the beliefs and stories we have about ourselves, our lives and our relationships. These can cause us to believe our "wants" are a part of an impossible fairy-tale dream that doesn't really happen to people "like us."

The relationships we have around us are a reflection of the love, or lack of love, that is flowing within. That is the truth. Getting real about what's happening means we tap into our core and get to the truth of the reasons why there's a contradiction between what we want and what's actually happening. This will help us realize why we aren't getting what we want and instead have created a belief or story (true or false) about the reason for it.

It's definitely easier to tell a story instead of taking responsibility, right? I mean, I definitely thought so. I know personally it would have been easier for me to blame what I went through in my life for the reasons I wasn't achieving the things I wanted most.

What did I want?

Well … everything, duh! I wanted to be happy, successful and in love. You know, the norm, but in some way shape or form, we all want to achieve the same feelings. Yes, happiness is a feeling. A feeling we can achieve every day. Success is a feeling, a feeling we can achieve every day. And love? Well, love is the ultimate goddess of feelings but another feeling we can feel every day. For one, love is who we are and why we are here. That I know for sure.

The difference between us is in how we achieve these feelings. How you feel happiness is completely different from how I feel happiness, and how success feels to you is different from how I feel success. How you feel love is different from how I feel love. Regardless of the differences in how we experience our emotions, why should we go a single day without feeling them? We shouldn't, but here's why getting real matters.

Although we might ultimately want to feel love, our meaning of love might be tainted by what we have experienced in our past, and that's incredibly important to understand. Why? Because if you are coming out of a toxic relationship hoping to focus on "loving yourself" (as beautiful as that sounds), then you will have a really hard time for one of two reasons:

1. You have a tainted perception of what love really is.

2. You believe love is outside of yourself and that in order to "focus" on it you have to "fix" yourself.

If we continue to believe that we have to fix ourselves, like we are a bird with a broken wing, then we will never really understand the power we have inside that is fueled by love. That love is already in us and all around us.

Now let's talk about why all this matters in our relationships.

Remember I said, "The relationship we have with ourselves sets the foundation for the relationships we will have with others"?

That means we are the powerhouse of everything that surrounds us. Once we begin to take responsibility for that, we are able to start allowing room for happiness to fill our lives.

Getting real puts us in our truth. It turns us into the scientist of our life, allowing us to see what's working and what's not working based on what is true right now.

Why is becoming a scientist important? Because scientists are constantly testing. They don't get attached to one specific way of achieving a theory. When one hypothesis doesn't work, they test a new one. When that fails, they test a new one, and a new one and so on and so forth. They don't create a permanent belief (theory/law in the science world) because something failed. On the contrary: failure is part of their job, and it certainly doesn't stop them from trying again.

So how does all this relate? For the sake of this science talk, I want you to imagine our beliefs about our life as laws. How many times have we formed a law in our life without testing a different hypothesis?

Let's take some examples and maybe you can find yourself in one of them. (By the way, these are made-up names and not actual stories.)

Suzie has been in and out of countless bad relationships that has led her to believe all guys are the same. (Law created.)

Nicole was told by her mother that she was a nuisance and a disappointment, which keeps Nicole walking on eggshells with people and believing she is not worthy of love. (Law created.)

Sarah was physically abused by her father growing up and although she doesn't necessarily think abuse is right, she still believes love comes with great pain, which keeps her in a verbally and emotionally abusive relationship. (Law created.)

Heather was told at a very young age to never depend on a man for happiness, and now she believes that having a relationship will only slow her down. (Law created.)

Deborah has been overweight her whole life and now believes she will never be able to lose the weight she desires. (Law created.)

Ashley grew up without money or material goods and realized how unhappy and stressed her parents were. Since then, Ashley has created a belief that money and material goods make people happier, which has led to her working so hard for all that she has but is still leaving her unhappy. So now she works even harder for more money and more things. (Law created.)

Not one of these beliefs these women created stemmed from an untrue story. The story of how these beliefs got created was very true for each of them. But the conclusions, beliefs and laws the women created from these stories are not true and are what could be causing them to feel stuck in certain (important) areas of life.

We have to get to the bottom of what our beliefs are because they can do a lot of damage without our even knowing they are there. This can cause us to be rigid, inflexible and unable to adapt, and in order for true happiness to fill our lives, we have to detach ourselves from anything that is keeping us restricted or is incongruent to our being.

How do we do that? You gotta get real, girl!

As self-help guru Tony Robbins says, "Divorce the story and marry the truth." That's where we need to start first. Ask yourself:

1. What is your story?

2. What law or belief came with that story?

3. What has this law or belief cost you?

Next, become a scientist. Ask yourself:

1. How could you test the story that has caused you to create the theory or law about how life works?

2. What are you willing to try differently?

3. How do you want to feel every day?

4. Are you willing to detach yourself from the stories that aren't serving you so you can live a life that is congruent with your truth?

5. What new story do you need to tell yourself so that you can feel HOT in every aspect of your life?

Once you have answered these questions honestly, you have taken the first step to becoming happy, open and trusting.

You can't live a positive and fulfilled life when your world is clouded by people who don't see what's better.

Two

Learning to Value
Your Values

An appalling truth I've realized is that we often devalue ourselves into the arms of the wrong relationship. The wrong job. The wrong friends. The wrong beliefs. The wrong situations. Catch my drift? And more often than not, we don't even know why. But let me share something I was told by a wise and very dear friend years ago. He said, "You are the bus driver of your life: Who gets on the bus, what gets on the bus and why they get on the bus are completely under your control."

I remember taking that message to heart because it meant I had to take responsibility for all the pain I was feeling. That everything—good and bad (mostly bad at that time)—was all caused by me. I don't know about you, but that was a painful realization for me. I mean, who wants to take that kind of responsibility?

So that means the bad relationships, the people I thought were using me, not being able to save my money, working overtime because I couldn't say "no," the not-so-good friends, the unfortunate situations I got myself into that (I thought) were outside of my control were all *me*?

I really tried to dodge that truth, but it hit me square in the nose, and hard! So hard, in fact, that I also cried hard. It wasn't the cute cry, either. I'm talking the snot out my nose, mascara running down my cheeks, hyperventilating type of cry. You would have thought my friend actually hit me with a ton of bricks because that's how it felt.

I have always said that words have power, and in this case, I was very thankful, because his words really struck a chord in me. Why? Because it left me confused.

Did you know that confusion really is the best place to be? It allows our mind to be open. There is no "absolute" in confusion. There's actually a beautiful sense of authenticity that lives in confusion because it opens up the possibilities of what could come. "Confusion" allowed me to stop and question. Question the people I allowed in my life. Question the behaviors I allowed of myself. Question the things I often complained about but did nothing to improve. Question my comfort with comfort. And questioned my inability to see what was actually going well for me.

The truth was, I was so consumed in what wasn't working in my life that it was hard for me to see what the reality was. The reality that said, "I am the cause of everything good and everything bad in my life," and the bad was caused by not "valuing" my values. More on that in a minute.

I remember I would take what sounded good over what actually felt good because I was just so scared that what felt good to me wouldn't be approved by others. I greatly feared rejection. Rejection meant that I wasn't good enough, and if I wasn't good enough, then I pretty much failed life. I would rather be seen for what others wanted to see than be seen for who I really was. I would think, "What if they don't like what they see? What if they don't see my worth? What if they don't value who I am? What if I'm just not enough?"

I was a professional people pleaser, and pleasing others made it easier for me not to focus on what was really important, like my own needs and what I valued most. It also kept me as far away from rejection as possible because as long as I wasn't being me, then how rejected could I actually feel?

As much as I felt like I was protecting myself, I also felt completely exhausted because I wasn't valuing who I was at all, and in the end, I was attracting people who didn't value me either. The standards we uphold in our life are a reflection of how much we value our values. If we aren't valuing the things most important to us, then our standards for how others show up in our lives aren't going to be very high. When you don't value yourself, the wrong people will come along and believe they don't have to value you either.

I was attracting things that didn't feel good because I wasn't being congruent with my truth. (That's a fancy way of saying that I wasn't being real.) When we aren't "real," how can we possibly be happy? We can't! Being real means we uphold what we value most in life, but that can be hard if we don't know what we value.

If I were to ask you what you value most in life, would you be able to answer? We can probably list a few things quickly, such as love, family, success and happiness, but do we actually live congruent to those values? Most of the time we do not.

When you don't value yourself, the wrong people will come along and believe that they don't have to *value you either.*

The best attention you will ever receive is the attention you *give yourself.*

I once asked someone what her values were and, no joke, she said "happiness," but she couldn't have been more unhappy in her life at the time. You can't say something is your value if you don't value it, and if it really is part of your values, then you can see right away that not valuing your values will create a contradiction in your life that may not feel too good.

Another example of this is saying that "health" is one of your values when how you've been actually living isn't, in any way, reflective of what health feels like. Does that mean "health" isn't really something you value? No, not necessarily. But if it is something you value, and you aren't upholding that value, then you can understand why you might feel unhappy most of the time because there's a contradiction between your truth and how you are actually living.

It's also not enough to know *what* we value without understanding how we *feel* those values. For instance, if "health" is one of your values in life, then how does it feel to be healthy? If "love" is one of your life values, then how does love feel to you, and in what ways can you achieve this value every day? If "success" is one of your values, define what success means so you know how to achieve it daily. It is really important for us to become clear about what our values actually are and how we can honor them because the more we live disconnected to them, the unhappier we will be.

Our values are key indicators of what inspires us. They are a gateway to how we, as individuals, operate. Everyone is different, and even though we may value the same things, how we fulfill those values will be completely unique.

Values really are the core of who we are. Some of the biggest spiritual leaders of our time speak of our core as the "truth of who we are," our "inner guidance system" or even our "internal compass." Why? Because our values want to guide us to what's really important, but if we don't even know what our values are and what we need to do to feel them, then we are going to constantly be in "seeking mode," and will be seeking the wrong things to make us happy.

With that said, I'm going to take you through a practice I had to do in order to get connected to what was true for me. Values are like blueprints to your life, and if you don't know them, you will continue to be lost and disconnected. So let's do a practice together, because we first need to know what our values are before we go any further.

The Practice: What Do You Value Most?

1. Get a pen and some paper (a journal, preferably) and let's go through this together.

Write a list of 10 to 20 things that you value most. (For example: love, success, relationships, money, courage, strength, health, peace, honesty, confidence, connection, friendship, laughter, growth.)

2. Circle the five values from your list that are most important to you.

3. Rank these five values on a new sheet of paper with #1 being the most important.

4. For each value, write three ways you feel them. Here's an example:

NICOLE'S VALUE LIST

#1. Love

When I can use my love to give to others.

When I eat dinner with my family.

When I hear an inspiring story.

#2. Courage/Strength

When I am able to try something new.

When I face at least one of my fears.

When I say something that's hard to say but needs to be said.

#3. Relationships

When my friends and I are spending time together.

When I share stories with my significant other.

When I'm working on a project with my peers.

5. Notice on Nicole's list, each of the three ways she feels her values contains the word "I." That is because we ideally want to make it very easy to achieve our top values without depending on someone else or something else.

So, now that we understand what values are important to us, the next question is how do we make sure we are constantly "valuing" our values? Because the truth is, we've always had these values, right? We just weren't paying attention to them, which is what gets us into trouble. Now it's time to understand the three ways you can start valuing your values.

THREE WAYS TO "VALUE" YOUR VALUES

1. Give yourself the gift of unconditional love. You can't really uphold the values you hold with other people if you don't respect and love your own values. Love is not just a value but also a feeling. We often search to gain the love and respect of another so we can feel good without doing the work of truly loving ourselves. Love is the foundation on which everything is built, and if love is not flowing internally, we will never value all that we are.

2. Don't settle. You know when you're settling. You will feel a misalignment with your spirit, causing you to disrespect your wants and needs. When we settle, we start to adopt the value system of others. And that's definitely not what we want, especially when those people don't respect their own values. Don't settle with friends, with lovers, with family and even with yourself. Also, never discount the things that are important to you.

Now here's the important one:

3. Be yourself! I often say, "Stop trying to *find* yourself and just *be* yourself." This may sound woo-hoo, but we have been conditioned at a very early age to take on the beliefs, stories and behaviors of others, starting with our families. Here's the problem, and often a bit of a catch: We love to be in search mode because it's actually easier than the state of being.

Searching means we rid ourselves of the responsibility for the way we are currently. It means that if we are *trying* or *finding* we are in seeking mode, when in reality, we either do something or we don't.

It gets even more crazy.

Have you ever tried to pick up a chair? If I asked you, "Try to pick up the chair next to you," could you? More than likely you would either pick it up or not. But "trying" means we are not responsible for the results. Same with "finding." If we are trying to "find" ourselves, then there is no responsibility for the time it takes for us to actually ... find ourselves.

Sounds like a mind twister, right? But the truth is, it's much harder to *be* yourself than to *find* yourself because it means you have to fully accept how you are now, in this very moment, flaws and all. It means that you have to continue to grow in order to develop, and growth is often uncomfortable because who you are is constantly changing. It means that you have to take responsibility for the decisions that you make when you are consciously making them. Definitely not easy, but absolutely crucial to your overall fulfillment and happiness.

And we're about that HOT life, aren't we?

Our values lead to a much larger discussion, but they set the standard of everything else we will be discussing moving forward. I know this personally, because it was the absolute first step to becoming connected and authentic to what was true for me.

"To love me first. It's not selfish to do that, but more rather common sense."

—Lala Anthony

Three

Letting Go of Being the Victim and the Need to Be Right

There are three ways we ultimately destroy our relationships:

1. Being the victim

2. Needing to be right

3. Needing to prove ourselves

What I always say is, "When you let go of the need to prove yourself, life has a way of proving it for you."

I can't tell you how many women I've spoken with who in some way, shape or form still hold resentment for a past situation that keeps them feeling weak and undeserving. This belief is so incredibly dangerous to not only ourselves but also the relationships around us because as long as we feel powerless (victimized), we will continue to allow fear to run our lives. The worst part is that this kind of thinking begins to turn into a pattern of how we exist and will trickle into our relationships.

For instance, let's look at Belle's story. Belle was a young girl who unfortunately (or fortunately, based on your perception) had to grow up fast. She was expected at a young age to raise her sister while her young mother battled the demons of her past. Often she was left at home by herself with her sister and had to take care of the motherly duties for this baby. At the time, Belle didn't think she was too young; she just did what was expected of her because her baby sister depended on it. There was little appreciation coming from her mom; instead, Belle was often the subject of physical and verbal abuse when her mother was feeling hurt or in pain. Belle was confused as to why she was punished so much when she thought she was doing what she was "supposed" to do.

It was very hard for her to speak up to her mom, even though she understood how wrong and unfair her mother's behavior was, until one day, she stood up to her mom for the first time ever ... which didn't end very well. She was severely punished for it, and although a part of her felt stupid because she knew what the consequences would be and still did it, she also felt a sense of justice (to stand up for herself and make right). Justice that, at the time, gave her the courage she needed to accomplish the things she did in her life.

A sense of justice is a good thing, and courage is absolutely necessary to stand up for how we should be treated, but there is such a thing as too much "justice" that certainly can keep us playing the victim card. But before I get into that, let's get back to Belle.

Belle ended up moving in with her dad, which was a good thing, but that need for correcting the injustices of the world was still in her (justice meter). Her justice meter certainly helped her when choosing solid people in her life and moving on from relationships that didn't serve her, but she still held on to anger and resentment from the injustices that happened to her when she was younger. Although this feeling didn't consume her entirely, it certainly stopped her from being truly happy because she felt skeptical, scared and unsure of herself around people, even though she knew how to make face pretty well.

Although she had an on-and-off relationship with her mom throughout her young adult years, she started to see a new conscious shift in her mom as she tried to become the mother she hadn't been during her daughter's young life. As beautiful as that was for her mom to grow, Belle couldn't find it in her to accept her mom in a new light because she was still holding on to the story of her past. And in her story, her mom was the villain and she, well, she was the victim.

That was the story she held on to her whole life, and this gave her significance and made her accomplishments seem that much more miraculous because it was a true story of heroics for her, but the truth was, that story was different. Her mom was different, and the more Belle held on to that story, the more her mother also had to live in the past of what she'd done.

That hardship you are going through right now is making you stronger. Don't crumble, it's showing you your power.

I'm gonna take a shot at what you're thinking. You are probably thinking, "Well, Belle isn't ready to forgive her mom and she shouldn't forgive her just because her mom wants her to." Trust me, I thought the same. Why? Because Belle was me! I couldn't fool you for too long, but here is the truth. I actually thought I had forgiven my mother. The primary reason I allowed our relationship to be "on" again was because I let the past hurts go (or so I thought). That was, until I noticed that I would punish her for every little thing.

If she got snippy because she was having a bad day, as we all do, I would react by cutting her off (justice meter). If her feelings got hurt because of something I did, I felt as if she didn't have that right because she still had years to make up to me before she ever had the right to express how she felt. Why? Because I was still the victim. But here's where that led us … nowhere! It didn't make me feel good, and it certainly kept her stuck reliving all of her mistakes.

We both weren't happy being around each other because there was no empathy or understanding for each other's situation. I wanted her to feel unbelievably sorry and regretful, which I knew she did, but how many times does someone need to show you until it becomes a chore, an obligation and completely unnecessary? Well, let's switch the story a bit here.

Have you ever done something in your life that you regret? Maybe you regret something you did when you were younger. Acted like a knucklehead at times. Hurt people you loved—maybe not intentionally, but still hurt them in some way. Did you get into trouble and cause a major headache for your parents or the person who had to bail you out? Have you said something that was spiteful and fucked up that thinking about it now makes you cringe?

Now answer this question: Are you a bad person?

No! You are not! You reacted because of how you felt at the time, and sure, you may have hurt someone's feelings while you were being a jerk or completely careless, but that's not who you are. That is how you acted temporarily. Now, what if one of those people in your life decided to punish you for the rest of your life because of the hurt you caused them? Would you think you deserved it? Would you continue having them in your life knowing that you would have to prove yourself every day to them? Wouldn't that be exhausting, and wouldn't you just relive your past idiocy every time you were around them?

That wouldn't feel that great, would it? Not to mention, what kind of flourishing relationship would that be? Well I'll just tell you that it wouldn't be a flourishing relationship at all, because all beautiful and sustainable relationships come from a place of love, and how much love do you think can flow through a relationship that has to play "make-up" for the rest of its days? That kind of relationship doesn't really allow for that type of flow.

Now, I'd like to ask you, is there a relationship in your life you feel victimized by? I know that word can seem a bit extreme, so if it does, is there an event that happened in your life you just can't seem to let go of? Maybe an event that included someone you cared about, and no matter how hard you try to let it go, the justice meter inside of you won't?

I knew a lady who asked how she could forgive her husband after an affair he had. She said that they were working on things now and trying to rebuild the trust, but at times she still felt betrayed and hurt. For those of us who've had a partner be unfaithful, you know that this feeling is on it's own fucked-up level.

Before I give any advice, I like to ask more questions, so I asked more about her relationship, such as what kind of connection they had before his unfaithfulness and how she would describe his character. I think asking about someone's character is important because it allows us to get clear on patterns. Patterns make up someone's character, but often we dismiss and ignore negative patterns for our own egocentric reasons, and then we become surprised when this person does an act of "betrayal."

However, when I asked her about his character, she said nothing but good things. They had a wonderful relationship. He supported her with anything and everything she wanted to do. He was a man of his word (you might question this now, but I will bring it back in context). He helped support his family. He made her feel safe, loved and understood, so why the betrayal?

When I asked whether there had been any recent changes in their life, she said, "Yes, I started a new business, so it has been a very busy time for me. There were times my husband and I would go days without really seeing each other. He was very supportive during my hectic times because he knew this was my dream, but I will be honest, I was not the nicest, and there were many dinners and dates he planned that I flaked on because I really wanted to give my business the attention it deserved. But just because I am focusing on a business, does that mean he can go and cheat on our relationship? I just don't think that's right. He showed no care for me or respect for what we have and knew this would kill me and still did it. Now I question my whole relationship. I don't know if he ever was a good husband now. I can't believe anything he says …"

Notice that I only asked whether there had been any recent changes prior to the cheating, and she went full circle, from praising his character to questioning their entire relationship. Do we blame her? No! But let's take a closer look at this. She went from being absolutely truthful and real about what their relationship was like to quickly questioning what she might not know. Again, this is not something we blame her for feeling, but let's take this a little deeper.

Because she said, "I can never believe anything he says," I asked her simply, "Is this true?"

She said, "Is what true?"

"Do you actually think you couldn't believe anything he says from now on?"

She replied, "Well ... I mean ... not really."

I replied, "Exactly, because if we were being real, you wouldn't be committed to saving this relationship if you truly felt he was untrustworthy, right?"

"Right," she said.

Okay, so that was the time we got real, which we talked about in the previous chapter, but now we had to get into what her values were so she could start to rebuild herself. The truth is, it's not enough to want to "save" your relationship. Relationships don't need you to do it any justice and make up for past wrongs. Instead, it needs you to bring your best self forward, and in order to do that, you must realign yourself with your truth. We can pick at her husband's flaws, his mistakes and what we think about his mistakes all day, but that won't change anything. Why? Because being the victim makes the other person the victimizer, and what the hell kind of relationship is that? Not a good one, I assure you, because how long will he have to make up for his bad decision? Well, if it were up to her, forever, but is that really going to make for a healthy, fulfilled, passionate, sustainable relationship? Probably not.

So now what? Should she forgive him? I know I'm giving you twenty questions, but I'm seriously asking you.

FORGIVENESS TRUTHS

Here's my take on forgiveness:

- Forgiveness is beautiful, but for most of us, forgiveness can often feel like an expectation or a task we have to do in order to be a "better" person. I definitely believe in the power of forgiveness, but I am also saying forgiving someone might be a tall order, especially in the midst of pain, unless you realize you are not the victim.

- Forgiveness is only hard when you attach yourself to pain and believe you have no power.

- Forgiveness is about reclaiming your power because your truest power comes from love. Love is what sees the bigger picture.

That doesn't mean everyone who has done you wrong deserves to be in your life. In order for you to truly be happy, open and trusting, peace must thrive, and in order for that to happen, love has to fill your soul through understanding.

Let's go back to the lady dealing with infidelity. She had already made the choice to stay with this man and felt deep down that this was the right choice, but she struggled with forgiveness. Even though she thought the act of staying with him was forgiving him, it wasn't. Again, you don't get brownie points for trying to do the "right" thing. In fact, you don't get brownie points at all in relationships. The very thought of being "right" creates hierarchy in the relationship and forces unnecessary expectations onto the other person. In this particular case, I can see she truly wanted to stay with him because the truth in her soul was wiser than she could comprehend at the time. She knew he fucked up, and in some small way she saw how she had contributed to the mistake, but as soon as that truth came out, she made the victimizing story her reality because she didn't want to be wrong.

In order for her to truly forgive him, she had to tap into her storage of love. She needed to rebuild the disconnect this pain had caused her. In order to restore any relationship, you need to be completely filled up within. Why? For two reasons:

1. For you to make the best decision possible for yourself

2. For you to be full-hearted in your relationship

The number one concern I hear from people is, "I can't just let them get off scot-free without any repercussions!"

Newsflash! It is not your job to parent an adult you choose to have a relationship with. The need to play justice system in our lives keeps us miserable and unhappy because it keeps us holding on to pain and expecting others to make it up to us, knowing damn well they will never make it up in the ways we want them to.

I know this very well because I held on to this ideal of how my mother should be and every time I was severely disappointed—not because she wasn't enough, but because I felt she wasn't doing enough. She was doing the best that she could, but it wasn't good enough to make up for her past wrongs. But then I started to see things more clearly through a practice I am going to show you now.

The Practice: Ho'o Pono Pono Prayer

I was shown this practice by a coach I had for a short while. Yup, even as a coach I have my own coaches and mentors, and she really came at a beautiful time. Timing really is perfect if you allow yourself to see it that way. Anyway, she introduced me to an old Hawaiian prayer called the Ho'o Pono Pono prayer, which means "To Make Right."

This prayer has four parts:

1. I'm sorry.

2. Please forgive me.

3. Thank you.

4. I love you.

She said, "I want you to write the prayer to your mom." I literally almost fell out of my chair!

"Why would I have to say sorry, please forgive me, and thank you? She's the wrong one here!" I said. Notice I'd made myself the saint and the right one in our relationship.

My coach continued, "The best way to clear resentment, frustration and anger is through love and vulnerability, to take responsibility for your own wrongdoing in the relationship."

What?! I thought I was perfect!

It took me a while to write that prayer, not because I couldn't find the words to say but because I wanted to hold on to my resentment. It became part of my identity so much so that I felt taking responsibility for my part of it would make her less wrong. Then I realized how wrong that actually sounded.

The other side of this practice is that I had to write one from her to me as if she were asking for forgiveness. The reason for this is because there are times we are left holding on to pain from someone who may not be in our lives anymore and we may never hear them say the words we need to hear for our soul to be healed.

When I show you the prayer I wrote to my mom, think of someone that you can do this prayer for. Is there a parent, significant other, family member or even stranger who has hurt you and you feel you have held on to that pain, not being able to truly forgive? Is there something you have done to someone and may want to ask for forgiveness but are unable to physically ask him? Or maybe it's something you've done to yourself. This prayer works for all of the above.

Hello Mom,

I know we haven't talked in a while, but I wanted to take the time to tell you how much you mean to me and apologize for a few things that I realize I have contributed to the distance of our relationship.

I apologize for making you feel like I didn't love you, with either the way my tone may have been to you or the way I talked about you to others. I know you must have heard the resentment in my voice throughout the years, even during the time our relationship was good. I didn't mean to cause you pain. I am so sorry for this, Mom. What can I do to make this action better for you? I love you.

I apologize for outcasting you at times when it came to my other family, and making you feel like you didn't exist, when I did and still do think of you every day. I am so very sorry, Mom. What can I do to resolve this pain I have caused? I love you.

I apologize for words that were exchanged the last time we talked. I took what you said literally, even when I knew you didn't mean it that way. I looked after my ego before your feelings. Again, I am so sorry, Mom. How can I make this better? I love you.

I want to also take this opportunity to thank you for my life as well as the life of my sister. She truly is a gift. Caring for her has made me the person I am today, and the reason I want to follow my passion for helping people.

Thank you for our movie nights when we were younger. It was some of the times I cherished and looked forward to most.

Thank you for our fun times and in-depth conversations when we were in a good space. I learned so much from you and I am so happy to have beautiful memories with you.

I love you, Mom, and always will.

Words don't mean anything if your energy can't back it up.

I don't know about you, but I believe in energy, and there was something about that prayer that felt like I let go of the restrictions and expectations I had about myself and my mom. I felt free and more connected to my truth because my truth was love. I loved my mom deeply, and I just needed to let go of being the victim, blaming her or making her "wrong." This exercise released in me the energy to truly feel authentic in who I am supposed to be, which was and always will be someone who loves, and it released the energy needed to allow my mother to be the person she is supposed to be now. It allowed her to make amends not because I expected her to but because she was being who she wanted to be, which happens to be the mother I've always needed her to be.

When we take away the need to make someone else wrong and let go of the attachment we have to the pain that was inflicted in the past, we allow ourselves to be who we need to be and others to be who they need to be. And if who they need to be doesn't align with our truth, we can still lovingly wish them well.

Oh, if you're wondering about the lady and her husband, they were able to rekindle their love, trust and passion in the relationship by understanding each other's needs and coming from a place of love, which is a daily practice for them and should be a daily practice for us all.

Four

Can We Get a Few More "Noes" in Our Vocabulary?

I'm going to introduce you to a new word that doesn't get as much credit as it deserves, especially since this simple word, if not used in the right way, can cause a lot of grief, anxiety and disharmony.

This powerful word is "no."

I've had a tough relationship with the word "no" throughout my life because I believed it was just so unlikable. I felt it disappointed people to hear the word "no," and why would I want to disappoint people? I wanted to make them happy, and if I made them happy, then I was worthy of being liked, and being liked meant I was "good enough." This belief turned into a disease. A disease that left me addicted to the approval of others.

Pleasing people became a distraction from myself. As long as the spotlight was on others, I would seem whole. People wouldn't be able to see the help my soul was crying for. As long as I felt put together amidst the chaos in my life, that was all that mattered, and in order to feel put together, I had to be everything for everyone. Yes, yes, yes, yes, yes and the only "no's" that came out were for the things that were important to me. No, to all the things I really wanted to do. No, to all that was important to me. No, to my time. No, to my relationships. No, to my health but yes, to you and yours.

I had to check myself into YA (Yes-aholics Anonymous).

"Hi, my name is Christal Fuentes and I have the disease to please."

This disease had left me feeling like my needs didn't matter. Like my only purpose on earth was to be liked. It had stopped me from pursuing my real desires because my desires could be offensive to others if their needs were put to the side. I became the "go to" for everyone. Why? Because the likelihood of me saying "yes" was pretty high. I mean, I'll be real, it was about a 95 percent shot I would say "yes" and the other 5 percent I'd say no was because I had already committed to someone else at the same time, and most of the time I would still make it work. God forbid I disappointed someone. I didn't want them to think I was too good for them or that their needs weren't important, and I sure as hell didn't want them to dislike me. So, yes, I will take you to your doctor's appointment even though I know you wouldn't do that for me. Yes, I will help you move because your close family and friends won't. Yes, I can spot you a couple of dollars here and there (and never get paid back). Yes, I have time to hear you cry about your fifth breakup with the same guy. Yes, yes, yes, yes, yes! ... But did I have time to go to the gym? No. Did I have time to organize my bills and get checks sent out? No. Did I have time to get my work done? No. Was I able to focus my time on a project I was super passionate about? No.

I saved up all the "noes" for me and all the "yeses" for everyone else, but it didn't matter as long as I was liked. I was drained waking up most days because I had no energy left for myself, but it didn't matter as long as I was liked. I neglected all the things that were really important to me, but it didn't matter as long as I was liked. I made myself sick because I didn't take care of my health, but it didn't matter as long as I was liked. The time I did have for myself I filled up with partying and drinking, but at least I seemed fun.

I gave more thought to how everyone else felt instead of how I was feeling that it truly became an addiction. However, I rationalized it by thinking I was doing it for the good of others even though I felt empty, depleted, fragile and scared to live my truth. Living my truth would have meant I would be seen as weak and not "put together."

I didn't just say yes to people. I said yes to insignificant things that took away my time, like watching trash TV instead of going to the gym. Playing on social media for hours on end instead of reading the book I'd been wanting to read. Picking up the tabs at dinner with friends instead of saving my money. Everything I did came from a place of wanting to numb myself from living a true life. As long as the spotlight wasn't on what I wasn't, I had fleeting moments of happiness but never really felt good unless I was numbing myself. Saying yes to everyone and everything else and saying no to what was important for me kept me from living authentically and feeling truly happy, and I rarely trusted people because I never gave them the opportunity to care for me.

Say no to one thing today that doesn't *serve you.*

Today I give myself permission to
_____.

For some reason, it's so hard for us to cater to our own needs first ... actually, I lie; I know the reason. We are taught to believe that taking care of ourselves first is a selfish quality, when in actuality, being selfish is the most unselfish thing you can be. Let's take that in a minute because I know there is going to be some rejection of the word *selfish*. It's just like that damn word *no*. It's so ugly and so...disappointing, isn't it? Well, we really need to change the meaning we have of these words because I'm going to give you a little newsflash. The very action of giving to others beyond your needs is absolutely fucking selfish. What?!

Yes, let me say that again, when we say yes to everyone but ourselves, we are doing it for some kind of gain. Perhaps it's to be liked more. Maybe it's to feel significant in someone's life, or perhaps it's to drown out what's really going on within ourselves. Either way, doing something to receive something else is (what I learned to call it) horse trading. We are giving for a return, and when we do that we give with expectation behind it. I don't know about you, but how many times have you been completely disappointed because you felt others didn't reciprocate what you did for them?

Go ahead and raise your hand because we've all been there. Expectation is the killer of joy and happiness. It is also the number one cause of stress and anxiety, but we will go into that deeper in the upcoming chapters. I just want you to understand how threatening it is to your happiness to fill up everyone else's cup besides your own.

I watched a wonderful video by spiritual coach Iyanla Vanzant (*love* her). She said, "When you put yourself last, you put God last because God is inside of you." I had to take the biggest breath in that moment. No matter what religious or spiritual beliefs you have, this statement is still a powerful one.

Let's imagine your bank account. Sorry to jump from God to your bank account. I can only imagine how that makes some of us feel! But for the sake of drilling this in, think about how much money you are allowed to take out of your bank account. Only what's actually in the account, right? Unless you are going to overdraw the account, which some of us do, but then you pay even more in overdrawn fees.

Well, this is exactly what we are doing in our relationships. We are giving beyond what we have in our account. We are giving too much time and energy that we are far in the negative. Then we expect to continue giving time and energy. News flash! We have to stop giving what we don't have. Why? Because we suppress our own happiness when we do that, and the very expectation that you will get a "return" on what you are giving will cost you your energy even more.

So back to the word *selfish*. I know you don't like it—trust me, I know—so I'm going to tell you what Iyanla calls it; she says it is really "self-full." That's a much better word, right? It means to give to yourself first. Because in order to be helpful to others (remember, help-FULL) we have to be full of love within ourselves.

The most powerful form of self-love is being able to say no to things that don't serve you. It means saying no when it doesn't feel good. Saying no when you mean no. The result is, your yeses will feel that much more empowering.

With that said, I must be truthful with you. There are some cons to this lifestyle. Practicing saying no in the beginning is no walk in the park. It is downright uncomfortable and may make you question yourself at first. You will think you are turning down opportunities and friendships and you will question your decisions.

"Friends" will drop out of your life because they won't think you are as "nice" as you once were. Family might discouragingly say, "You've changed," and you might feel more selfish instead of self-full, but guess what? The freedom you will feel shortly after is going to make you feel so much more empowered. It is going to make you feel confident about standing up for what you want and what's important. It is going to make you feel like your yeses are now backed with intention and aligned to your truth. You will see more quality people around you who value you and your time. These people will want to give to you, not out of expectation, but because they love you. They don't just like you because you're nice; they like you because you give full-heartedly and are a person of your word.

The first time I actually admitted I was a yes-aholic was when my hubby Andrew finally had a "come to Jesus" chat with me one night. He said, "Babe, why did you say you would help this person move tomorrow when you were already stressing about not having time to finish your work? You don't need to help this person if it's taking away from what you really need to do for yourself. She would've found someone without you, and that's okay."

I just cried like a baby for the next hour, mostly because what he said was right and also because I started feeling sorry for myself, not in that pitiful way, but because I realized I wasn't honoring my spirit. I realized I put myself last on the list of priorities, and that just wasn't right.

Since then, I made a promise to him and to myself that I would start honoring my truth more by saying what I meant to say instead of what people wanted to hear. Every day was a challenge, but I dared to brave through it. Every time someone asked me to do something I knew I couldn't do, I said "no." Every time someone called to use my time as a vent sesh, I said "no." Every time I was invited to something I knew wouldn't serve me, I said "no." Now, remember,

In life you will be questioned for your thoughts, your feelings, your passions, your friends, your decisions, your style choices, your eating habits, your love and your beliefs. But to change on behalf of another is when you start compromising the pieces of yourself that make you unique. Don't change to make someone else feel better, change to better yourself.

I said the practice doesn't just mean saying no to people. Saying "no" is necessary for some of the activities we allow ourselves to get consumed with, too. Remember I said I was getting consumed by trash TV when there were other things I needed to do with my time? We all have our guilty pleasures, but we have to leave them as pleasures instead of habits.

Saying "yes" had turned into my habit. A habit that cost me precious energy and clouded my perception of what was real.

I've definitely lost some people whom I thought were in my life for me but were only in my life for the conveniences I made in theirs, and I only have one thing to say: "Bye, Felicia!" Because the people I have near and dear to my heart are ones who value my time, my generosity and my interests.

So why is saying "no" so important, and why is it essential for your overall happiness? In order to truly feel happy, your spirit has to be full, and in order for your spirit to be full, you have to stop draining your energy with things that don't serve you, people that don't serve you and activities that don't serve you. A lot of times we don't even know we are saying yes to everyone and everything until we come home at the end of the day completely drained, but the need to be liked, praised and appreciated makes saying "no" a hard practice. For most of us, we are addicted. Raise your hand if you will be in the next session of Yes-aholics! See you there.

Now, I don't want you to think saying "no" is going to come easy. I'm sure you are already dreading it, but just in case you thought I was going to ease your worries ... I'm not.

Saying "no" is a practice, a practice that becomes a conscious decision every single day. Saying "no" doesn't mean you turn into the big bad Witch of the West, even if it feels like it the first few or hundred times, and I certainly don't want you to believe you have to turn into a Grinch in order to actively practice saying "no." Saying "no" just means you're telling the truth. You are telling the truth of what you are actually able to do. Like I said before, being selfish is the most unselfish thing you can be. When you put your needs first, you are able to offer better assistance to those around you. If you are giving assistance to those around you before yourself, then you are truly being selfish because helping and serving others will come with an expectation.

Remember what I said before, that the reason I kept saying yes to people was because of my selfish need to be liked, to feel good enough and to be worthy? Well, I tried so hard not to be selfish that in the midst of it all I became the most selfish person. Whew! Isn't that crazy?

Saying "no" is not an easy practice, especially if you're a person who has said "yes" most of your life. So I'm going to give you a few steps to get into a daily habit of saying more "noes" to those around you so that you can say more "yeses" to yourself.

The Practice: Can I Get a "No"?

1. Become conscious of how much time you have available for yourself. If you don't know how much time you actually have available for yourself, then it will be easy to say yes to people who will fill up your time for you. So do yourself a favor and fill in your own time before offering service to those around you.

2. Prioritize people in your life. It sounds rude, but it's not—it's necessary. Prioritizing people in your life allows you to organize the priority of needs and the time you have available. For example, your number one priority is to yourself, and if you have a significant other, he or she is number two. Knowing this allows you to first cater to yourself, because you need to and also because you will be a better and fuller partner to your significant other. It also helps you say no to other people who might be cutting into your priority slot and your significant other's priority slot. It allows you to be clear on what time and energy you have for the people and activities that matter most to you.

3. Practice saying "no" to one person or one activity a day. When you do that and feel badly, say "yes" to one thing that you can do for yourself that day instead.

If we want to be happy, open and trusting in our relationships, then we have to have the energy for our most important relationships. A lot of times I see women giving so much of themselves to everyone around them that they damage their most intimate relationships because they don't have the energy for those who matter most. We need to get back on track and understand who matters, and in order to do that we need to prioritize the people around us and the things that we are actually able to do.

So I ask you right now to think about your most important relationships, starting with yourself, and start allocating the time and the "yeses" necessary for those relationships. That way, it's easier to say "no" without feeling like a failure. Do this very same practice for the activities that you engage in every day that may or may not be serving you. If there are activities that you know should be a priority, make sure you say yes to them before committing to anything else.

If you practice saying "no" to what doesn't serve you and "yes" to the people and activities that matter most, you will notice drastic changes in your life in a positive way. You'll find the people you love most and that are most important will value your time and respect who you are. You will find time opening up for you. You will see an increase in productivity. Anxiety and stress levels will begin to fade. You will begin to feel freer, happier, more open to the blessings around you and more trusting of what's to come. And that's a beautiful feeling, isn't it?

Five

Stop Taking Things Personally; Nothing Is Personal

One of the most important things I've had to practice in my life—and let's just be real, it still is something I have to practice—came from a teaching by one of my favorite authors, Don Miguel Ruiz. He said, "Taking things personally is the maximum expression of selfishness because it makes the assumption that everything is about me."

Now remember what I said in the last chapter about wanting to please people? In the midst of becoming a "yes" person, I took everything personally; it just came with the territory. I couldn't feel good if others didn't feel good. How could I not take it personally if I couldn't make someone happy? How could I not take it personally if I knew someone was mad at me? How could I not take it personally if I knew I had disappointed someone?

The more I began to say "no," the more uncomfortable I became, because now people were upset and I felt like it had everything to do with me. Uncomfortably, I realized that the source of most of my unhappiness was fueled by taking on the emotions and behaviors of others. Now that I got the "no" part down, I had to learn that taking things personally will still destroy any chance at happiness. It is very difficult to be in a relationship with someone who has this mind-set.

Remember I told you about the difficult relationship I had with my mother? Well, I spent most of my young life believing I wasn't worthy of love because I took her behavior personally. I mean, how could I not? A mother-daughter relationship is pretty personal, right? Yes, I believe that it is, but why do we hold on to what someone has done to us as a child long into our adulthood? We only become attached to painful memories and stories when we have made it personal. That is what begins to dictate our beliefs about life, the world and our relationships, which ultimately causes loads of problems.

It took me a while to understand this because I constantly wondered why I was so frustrated when I was around her even in my adult life. It was because of the expectations I placed on her and what I felt she should be doing for me. How she should be making up for the past. How she should now be there for me. Even in my adulthood, I believed that her every action, in some way, reflected me. But that's all bullshit! The real truth is her behavior had nothing to do with me. It had everything to do with the pain, hurt and stories she had about herself and her life.

The mistake we make is believing that any one person has the power to dictate how we feel. We alone create our emotions, not others. Nothing is personal. Even if someone says that it is. Ohhh, this is tough, trust me, but it's one of the most important habits to rid ourselves of if we want to have love flow through the relationships that are important to us.

FAMILY MAY TEST YOU

The more I help women, the more I see that the major cause of disruptions in their relationships comes from taking things too personally.

There was one remarkable story I will never forget that was shared by one brave lady who asked me how to handle family members who disagreed with her decision to stand by her now-daughter, who at a young age had decided who she was and who she was meant to be, even though she wasn't born as a "she." This mother courageously explained to me the battle she was going through between respecting her family's beliefs and choosing to stand by her daughter, even though the backlash and the consequences meant her family might disown her. She recalled the hurt she felt when her family didn't respect her decision because it meant they didn't respect her daughter. I couldn't believe the vulnerability and the courage it took for her to seek my advice, especially with something so personal that society has made so taboo. She asked me how she could keep the peace with her family and their beliefs but still respect her daughter's decision for her life.

We all want to keep the peace with our family, especially the ones we love and the people who are closest to us. I sympathized with her desire to make her daughter's life full of love, happiness and respect, but still wanting to respect the beliefs that her family had about her decision. What we must understand, however, is that people have their own stuff, their own beliefs and their own stories about the world. Sometimes keeping the peace can be more disruptive to our soul when we try to control how everyone around us feels.

The need to dominate is the ultimate sign of *weakness.*

"The root of anything that causes pain is fear."

-Tandar Tanavoli

I could clearly see that her main frustration was that her family wasn't coming from a place of love. Instead, their beliefs were more important than making her and her daughter feel understood and supported. This is a very intimate story about the dynamic that happens with most families when they have disagreements. Everyone has his or her own outlook on the world. However, what we must strive to understand is that we have no control over how someone else feels. We only have control over what we allow around us.

The sad part is that most of us continue to be loyal to those who hurt us, even if they did so unintentionally. We are so loyal that we even take their hurts, their beliefs and their stories personally. You can't sustain a proper relationship while still being attached to that hurt and the stories they bring that are incongruent to who you are.

What this mother was ultimately trying to do was keep the peace between her family and her daughter, even at the expense of her sanity. The hardest thing to realize is that even the ones we love need a timeout sometimes. I truly believe that although we have no control over how others choose to behave and live their lives, we do have control over who and what we allow around us, even if it's close family.

My advice to this beautiful woman was to continue standing by her daughter's decision. Her daughter at a very young age chose fulfillment and to live authentically. And although those closest to them have lived their lives through their own stories and restricted beliefs, it is important for this mother to show her young daughter a new model of the world, one that lovingly respects those who may not agree with our life choices and just as lovingly chooses to honor their truth and spirit without taking their actions personally.

Again, this is a very hard practice. How could we not take what family members say and do personally? How can we not react when someone attacks us? It's not easy. But there's one thing that helped me. You want to know what that is?

Empathy. Empathy is the key to understanding others. I truly believe the biggest gift you can give yourself is the ability to put yourself in other people's shoes. So often we come across people who cannot do the same, and that is okay. But the ability to see what someone may not be seeing adds to overall understanding and allows you to detach yourself from what's not real. Because the truth is, nothing is personal.

When I became empathetic to my mother's story, my mother's perception of the world and her beliefs about life, I became less attached to how I thought she should behave and more conscious of how I reacted. Now I know I'm talking a lot about my mom, because the truth is she has become one of my biggest spiritual teachers. But this is just one relationship out of so many in my life where I've had to learn the same lessons that I talk about. I can't tell you how many times I've struggled taking things personally, even now in my intimate relationship.

There are so many times I take things personally even with my sister. And what I notice is if I do not catch myself in the act of this negative habit, I start to restrict the energy and love flowing between each of my important relationships. I start to see the people I love feel judged. I start to see their spirit dwindling because they don't feel "good enough" in my presence. When we take things too personally, we end up attacking. We attack because we do not feel good enough. And the truth is, you are more than good enough. And the people you love, regardless of how they show up, deserve your love and respect.

TECHNOLOGY, CELEBRITIES AND ATTACHMENT

Now, let's switch things up a bit. I talked about taking things personally in our intimate relationships, but let's address another phenomena I am seeing. Let's address media. There are many types of media, from social media, CNN, E! and MTV (even though I've yet to see any actual music), to my personal favorite, OWN network. Media is all around us and, good or bad, has the power to influence many of us.

I personally love technology and how it has allowed our world to come closer together and become more empathetic to those who may not be so near. However, in the midst of the good, technology can also be used for evil. I often see disruptive words send a ripple effect of negative energy throughout the web.

We have become so attached to how others live their lives, especially with well-known people like celebrities. We've become so attached to what we believe they're doing or not doing, how they should be acting, how wrong they are for living the way they live and what they should do with their bodies that it becomes a burden and a disruption in our own lives. I see so many hateful comments and posts shaming, condemning and belittling the lives of others as if these were "personal" relationships.

Why have we taken the behaviors of people we don't even know so personally? Let me use an example, from one of the most popular families we all know: the Kardashians. Now, for some, you may have already felt an immediate negative feeling, urge or emotion. If this is true, ask yourself why that is. The reason why I use this family as an example—besides the fact that they are one of the biggest families in the media—is because so many of us have "opinions" about them. Liking or disliking this family is not the issue. The issue lies with the attachment that comes from taking things so personally that it causes an emotional reaction. I use them as a small example because the reaction I often see to this family (mostly the bad reactions) is just a small window into the attachments we have to other things that could be causing us to be unhappy.

Again, I am a lover of media and technology because I see the good and because I am inspired by those who are living a fulfilled and happy life. I truthfully would not be doing what I do had it not been for a lot of women I see in the media today. How my fellow ladies want to dress, showcase themselves, live their lives, raise their families, do their business and expose themselves is not personal to me.

Once you let go of the need to take things personally and quit making it about yourself, you begin to release the control and attachment to things that are keeping you stuck and unhappy. What you will begin to see is something phenomenal—the freedom that comes with the ability to let go.

Remember as easy as it may sound, This. Is. Difficult! I can honestly say that this is something I have to practice daily, especially in my line of work. There have been many times when I became too attached to the outcomes of my clients' lives and whether or not they actually listened to my advice.

The closest relationships to us are the hardest because we always want to make sure that we are making people feel good around us, but the truth is, we have no control over how they feel. We only have control over how we feel and what we bring to the table. Everyone has his or her own emotions and no one person is in charge of another person's feelings. But when we actively take things personally, we become attached to the behaviors of others and their emotions and allow ourselves to believe that we can control them. But if we want to live a fulfilled and happy life (which is probably the reason you are reading this), then we must get ourselves in check. Our need for significance drives us to believe everything is about us, and it most definitely is not.

THE DRAMA WE MAKE UP IN OUR HEADS

How many times have you taken someone's vibe so personally that you scripted a whole scene of *Housewives* going down? Go ahead and raise your hand and I'll raise mine along with you, because I've been so guilty of this type of behavior.

Just recently, Andrew and I took twenty family members on a trip to Maui. Just in case you didn't read that correctly let me say that again, T-W-E-N-T-Y people! Twenty different personalities, twenty different wants and needs and twenty different problems. Luckily, the trip was amazing, but there were several times I had to check myself. A couple of times I temporarily thought people were mad at me because I sensed they were "disconnected" (term used by a coach who thinks *way* too much). In actuality, those family members were just tired from their sixteen hours of traveling. It had nothing to do with me except my need to be the center of attention (significance). No one was disconnected. No one was ungrateful, and no one was mad at me. I made all that up just by taking their vibe personally.

Yes, that is what you call cray cray!

We've all done that, right? Yes! We all do, and we have to stop it because it's restricting our spirit and freedom. Even if you are the reason someone is acting up, that is not your problem. They are in charge of how they feel, and you are in charge of how you feel. You can only make sure that you show up with empathy, understanding and love, and if you find that hard, well, then that is why I have just the practice for you.

The Practice: Compassion

What I ask of you now is to start your daily practice not just with your intimate and immediate family and friends, but also in the online world, as we are always online. The practice is to show compassion, understanding and love even when someone's life views are completely different than yours.

So let's think of a relationship right now where you know you could've caused some frustration, anger and pain even when you didn't mean to because you took things too personally. Perhaps it was an intimate partner, a family member or a coworker. It could even be someone you didn't even know. Once you have the relationship in mind, what do you see differently now that you didn't see before? What was it that you took personally and allowed it to affect your feelings and behavior? Ask yourself, was it even personal? Even if you still feel like it was, does that person really have the power to make you feel any way but how you want to feel?

Let me answer that for you: No, no one has that power. That is all you, girl! But we like to give our power away and play victim to the actions of others. One way to stop the victimizing mind-set is to stop taking what others say or do personally.

How do we do that? That's a great question, and the answer lies with some of the things we went over in previous chapters.

1. Let go of the need to prove yourself or the need to be right: Most of the reasons we get so attached to the things people do or say is because we want (in some way) to prove our worth, to be understood or to be right. Becoming happy, open and trusting in life and in your relationships requires you to detach yourself from the behaviors, perceptions and beliefs of others. You have no control over anyone except yourself.

2. Strive for empathy: Having empathy means you strive to understand the feelings of another person. If we had more empathy, we'd rarely take things personally because we would be able to put ourselves in the other person's shoes! Imagine how many arguments over small things would be eliminated if we showed more empathy for where someone is coming from, even if we don't understand it completely.

3. Show more love to yourself when you're most uncomfortable: The urge we have to attack or take things personally comes from a lack of love flowing internally, and as hard as this really is (trust me, I know), you must show the most love to yourself in the moments you feel it least. For instance, if someone says something that may be belittling, you do not—I repeat, *do not*—show love to yourself by attacking back. That does not come from a place of love—that comes straight from the ego—and if we are trying to build healthy relationships around us, there's no time for the ego to show its face.

Is this doable? It absolutely is!

Is this another hard practice? Yes, but 100 percent rewarding. If it were easy, we'd have a world filled with happy people and happy relationships (my dream!), but the truth is, it's equally hard to live in the negative patterns we've allowed into our lives, too. So the choice is yours! I choose and always will choose to be absolutely fucking HOT over anything else!

Six

Stress, Anxiety and All the Feelings That Suck!

We can't talk about happiness and the good feelings without discussing all the feelings that suck. As beautiful as it is to be happy, full of joy and passionate, it is equally beautiful to be able to feel the spectrum of the scale when it comes to feelings. Yeah, sure, being sad, depressed, anxious, stressed, angry or frustrated aren't the most pleasant of feelings, right? But without them we wouldn't appreciate when we actually feel good.

What I find is we usually have such a resistance to feeling negative emotions, when really our negative emotions have a lot to say about what's going on inside. We often don't know what's happening inside, but our most constant feelings are a gateway to the conflict between what our truth wants to feel and what's actually happening.

So many women I've talked to have experienced anxiety at one time or another. Just the thought of the word *anxiety* is enough to make one cringe. But even the feeling of anxiety is a symptom to a deeper dis-ease, a "dis-ease" that often goes without notice.

Have you ever asked yourself what was wrong when you're feeling stressed, anxious, sad or depressed but couldn't really put a finger on it? What I've noticed is that most of us growing up were never taught to truly understand the emotions happening within. Most of us have learned to suppress the negative emotions because they were "bad." But all that's done is allow us to stay unaware of why these feelings come up.

Somewhere down the line, in our inability to become aware and address the feelings that surface, we have simply learned to drug (numb) our emotions. Not just in the literal sense, but in behaviors we have learned that temporarily work to change our emotional state. There are so many "drugs" of choice, and no one is "better" than the other. It is important to understand our most common negative emotions, whether they are anxiety, depression, anger, frustration, sadness or stress, and become aware of how we might be drugging those emotions instead of getting to the root of what's actually happening.

One book I will always treasure reading is *10 Mindful Minutes* by Goldie Hawn. In it she discusses the importance of developing emotional skills at a young age in order to reduce stress and anxiety in our adulthood. This book was primarily written for parents who had young children and who wanted to instill a meditation practice that would bring connection and presence to their emotions and feelings. Although I am not a parent, I found this book especially useful for me personally and for what I do, because many of us did not learn emotional skills at a young age, and that is stopping us from feeling the way we want to feel.

The basic concept of this form of meditation is becoming aware of each emotion as it passes through. The problem we've created for ourselves is that by not fully understanding why we feel the way we do, we become attached to specific emotions more than others. And because some of these emotions don't feel good, we have also learned how to drug ourselves in the process. But before we get into how we most commonly drug ourselves, let's first understand our most common emotions and where they come from.

As I said before, emotions and feelings tell a story of what is happening within. Negative emotions are fleeting (as they should be), but they will stay if what caused them is not resolved. That's just not what we want, right? We want our positive feelings to be more constant and less fleeting, instead of the negative ones.

Let me tell you a personal story of a time recently when I began to feel increasingly anxious. I like to say "recently" because I want you to remember that although I help women in establishing healthy relationships through positive emotions, it doesn't make my battle with them any easier. Why? Because, well, I'm human, and no matter who you are, or what you do, there will be times you will experience discomfort.

Growing up, when times were tough and my mom was struggling, I fortunately had a very close relationship with all of my grandparents. Each grandparent took a strong role in raising me (alongside my father). I was particularly close to my grandfathers on both my mom and my dad's sides. In December 1997, I lost my grandfather (on my dad's side) unexpectedly. Luckily, I had a chance to say good-bye to him, but that didn't make it less painful.

Now, a lot of people might think, "People lose their grandparents all the time; that's what happens with old age." Yes, I understand that, but my grandparents were more than just grandparents; I truly believe they were my soul mates sent to me to be my guardian angels, and I particularly felt that way about my grandpa.

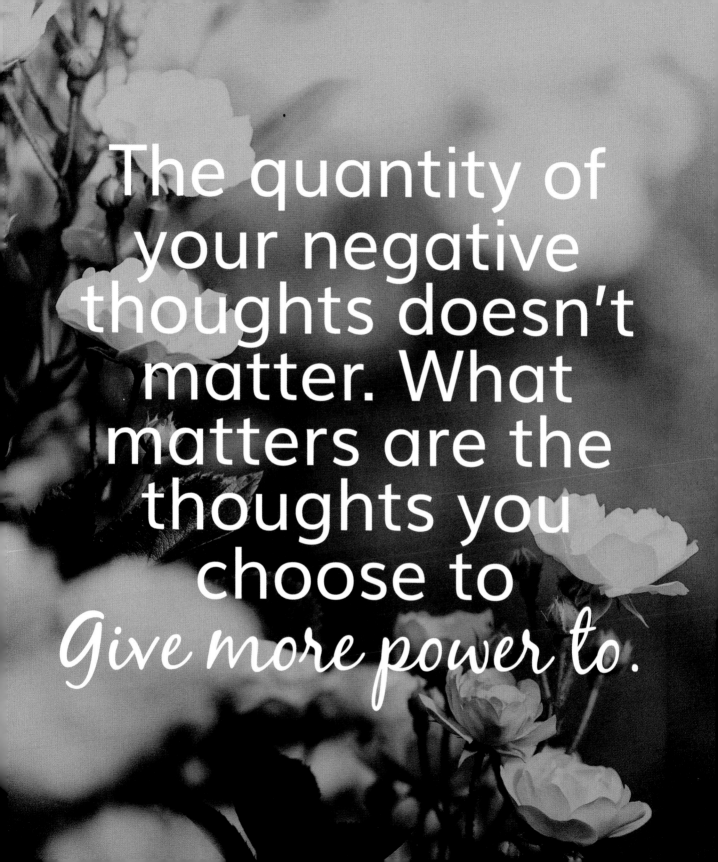

The quantity of your negative thoughts doesn't matter. What matters are the thoughts you choose to *Give more power to.*

If you want to find the bad, you'll find it. Same goes with the good.

What would you rather find?

After losing my grandfather, I started to grow distant from my grandpa on my mom's side without really realizing it. Throughout the years he had become increasingly sick with cancer, and I (ironically) had grown increasingly distant. Why would someone who is a relationship coach and who counsels people on how to develop sustainable relationships with family members contradict her own message by becoming distant to a relative who had mattered most to her throughout her life? I couldn't even answer that question until I started developing anxiety this past summer without knowing why.

Anxiety? I help women with managing their emotions and feelings! Why the hell would I, out of all people, feel anxious?!

I would wake up in the middle of the night with my heart pounding out of my chest as if I were having a heart attack. I'd have an attack in the middle of my day while writing blog articles on anxiety. I found myself exhausted early in the day without knowing why. Now, I don't know about you, but this wasn't looking too good, especially coming from someone whose job is to help others not feel this way.

I was starting to feel like a fraud because I couldn't understand my anxiety. I would cry to Andrew because I couldn't pinpoint where this feeling was coming from. I started to judge myself for feeling anxious, which, in turn, added more stress and anxiety. I would wake up feeling uninspired, restless and upset that I hadn't figured it out yet. And then one beautiful day I was in the kitchen with my girlfriend, and she witnessed me having one of my many anxiety attacks at that time. She took the time to truly listen with presence and understanding. I do believe you are sent certain people at specific times to help you just when you need it, and God knows I needed it.

She knew anxiety was a symptom of something happening within, because, well, we talk about feelings a lot. But truthfully, I was too embarrassed to even talk about what was really happening, even to a dear friend, because I have always been the rock for others and thought it would look weak for someone in my position to be feeling the way I did. Luckily, she didn't allow me the freedom to just walk away. Instead, she granted me permission and the space I needed in that moment to be vulnerable.

The first part of our talk was just me rambling, and she didn't interrupt; she stayed present. Again, she was listening to the things I said and also the things I didn't say. She asked questions that got me to focus on where my anxiety could be coming from until I started expressing my fears. One of those fears stems from an early age, and the reason why I had distanced myself from my grandfather was because I was scared to feel the same pain I had felt when I lost my other grandpa. Another fear came from the contradiction I felt between the values that I live, which is that relationships are everything, and the fact that I had managed to separate myself from a relationship that was important to me. The third fear was that I could lose my grandpa and not be able to make up for lost time and that I would live in regret. Whew! All of that came out in my rambling!

What I love about my girlfriend was that, instead of trying to make me feel better, she came from a place of deep wisdom and told the truth. There was no sugarcoating or doing what girlfriends usually do, which is to make the problem smaller than it is. Instead, she understood my fears and said, in so many words, "Yes, you can't make up for lost time and your distant relationship, but you can, at any point, start to build a relationship with him now. It doesn't matter what your expectations about the relationship are. You can, starting now, say whatever it is you need to say to him, no matter how ashamed or awkward you may feel. Christal, you may have let yourself down, and trust me, you have all the right to cry that out, but just remember, there is something beautiful that comes with feeling the things we don't necessarily want to feel because it prompts us to become more aware of the things that are important for us to change."

I can't tell you how much better I felt after that conversation with her, and it reminded me of something Brené Brown, author of three *New York Times* bestsellers, said about sharing your story with those who have earned the right to hear it. If you haven't read any of Brené Brown's books or watched her TED talk "The Power of Vulnerability," do yourself a favor and do that ASAP. She is an absolute must when it comes to learning the power of vulnerability, shame and trust.

But back to how the chat with my girlfriend had left me…. Now that I had finally gotten to the root cause of what I was feeling, it was my responsibility from that moment forward to do something about it. I couldn't contradict my values any longer, especially because I had become aware of it. This experience makes me wonder how many of us walk around not knowing why we feel the way we do, and instead of acknowledging our feelings, we find ways to numb that feeling. I'm not gonna lie: I totally understand why people would seek a pill, a drink or a doughnut to calm their anxiety, because what I felt at that time was more than I could bear. But here's the thing: if we are able to become "scientists" of our emotions, we will need to do less numbing and more healing.

So how do we do that? Well, like my girlfriend said, we have to appreciate the uncomfortable feelings and what they are calling out in us to change in order for us to feel the more abundant feelings. So I'm going to give you four ways to make peace with your most common negative (uncomfortable) emotions.

MAKING PEACE WITH SHITTY FEELINGS

1. Be aware of when these feelings happen. Don't get too attached to them, but become present to when they happen and see if you can catch the pattern of when and why they are coming out.

2. Acknowledge and forgive when you are having a fear-based emotion. It happens to everyone. We must forgive ourselves first for having negative emotions. They are serving a purpose, and our job is to understand their message.

3. Tell the truth. Allow yourself the gift of vulnerability. It is okay to feel these emotions; nothing is wrong with you, and you certainly don't have to hide them. This is just an opportunity for you to connect to your truth. You don't need to make this emotion smaller or bigger than it is, but just tell the truth of what you are feeling.

4. Give yourself love. Love makes everything better (as cliché as that may sound). Love also helps you see things more clearly. Love doesn't mean we have a pity party and become the victim; it means we see things how they are and accept them in that moment while knowing we are worthy of feeling better.

I want you to understand that negative emotions happen to everyone. I repeat, *everyone*. If you are human, you will experience negative emotions.

A lady once asked me why, after all the yoga, after all the spiritual practices that she did and the health shift she had made in her life, she still had spurts of negative emotions. My response was that negative emotions are a part of life. No matter how positive, successful, happy and content you are with your life, you will have spurts of negative feelings. What you don't want to do, however, is stay in the negative emotions. You want to be able to allow emotions to pass, but in order to that, you have to make peace with them. And that happens when you become aware of, acknowledge and forgive those feelings, telling the truth of what's really happening and giving yourself the gift of love. Only then will we be able to fully understand where they are coming from and allow them to pass peacefully.

And getting back to my client, it doesn't matter how much you think a spiritual practice is good for you; if it doesn't feel good, then you must change your practice. Yoga, meditation and crystals might work for others, but that doesn't mean they will work for you. Spiritual practices are not one-size-fits-all. Our spirits are uniquely different, and it is up to you to find a ritual or practice that suits your spirit most.

That's not to say that these practices will *never* suit you if they don't right now, but maybe at this stage of your life, something just doesn't work, and there's no shame in that. Also, they are called "practices" for a reason, so just because meditation and yoga may not feel right the first time you try them doesn't mean they're not for you. It's just like going to the gym: You have to create a ritual and a routine for it to start feeling good. But if after doing something for years you aren't getting the results you want or need to feel, then you have to be open to switching up the game. There's no use in doing things that give your spirit no joy.

So, after you make peace with your feelings, make sure you are checking your rituals and practices. Are they aligned with how you want to feel, or are you just doing them out of expectation? Really look at the patterns of your days, because usually there are small tweaks we can make that can drastically change our emotions.

Now, why is this so important to our relationships? First of all, our emotions play an important role in the connectedness we feel with ourselves. As I said before, the relationship you have with yourself sets the foundation for the relationships you have with others.

Once we get our emotions in check, we will feel more connected to the feelings we want to feel, and that is where abundance truly lives. That is when we have more energy to fuel the relationships around us and are able to be in charge of our own happiness, instead of expecting others to be the main source of our happiness. It also stops us from being in fear-based relationships (which I will talk about in upcoming chapters) and allows us to choose only great relationships that truly align with our values.

Don't take on the baggage of others, especially when you don't know how to *release your own.*

WHAT, HOW AND WHY

So what are your most common negative emotions? List at least three, and if you don't have a clue you can choose from the list below:

- Abandoned
- Abused
- Addicted
- Afraid
- Aggravated
- Aggressive
- Alone
- Angry
- Annoyed
- Ashamed
- Anxious
- Belittled
- Betrayed
- Bored
- Broken
- Burdened
- Chaotic
- Conflicted
- Confused
- Embarrassed
- Emotional
- Emotionless
- Fake
- Frustrated
- Grumpy
- Guilty
- Hateful
- Helpless
- Hopeless
- Negative
- Numb
- Overwhelmed
- Pain-wracked
- Panicked
- Paranoid
- Rageful
- Sad
- Stressed
- Suppressed
- Suspicious

Of course, this list contains just some examples of negative emotions and certainly may describe yours. I encourage you to really dig deep on some of the emotions you feel most often. How do you experience them? Do you close yourself off in a room? Do you down a huge brownie (raise my hand)? Do you go straight to the wine cabinet (raise my hand again)? Do you find yourself arguing more with the ones you love? Do you find simple pleasure or connection in "woe is me" behavior? This is a time to get truthful. Tapping into our behaviors through our most vulnerable states allows us to rewire what's not working for us.

Ask yourself, why did these emotions happen? Was there a specific event that occurred prior to these feelings? Did it start from a worry in the future or remembering something in your past? Was it something someone did or said?

Getting as specific as possible will give you more clarity about what is happening internally, which most of the time we are unaware of. And guess what? The things we are usually unaware of are exactly the things that stop us from having the life and relationships we want and deserve.

For real! Remember I told you about the period of time I was having anxiety attacks? On the surface I had no idea what was happening until I dug deep. Emotions always tell us what is happening internally. Just like diseases. Symptoms causing "dis-ease" are the body giving you a warning of what's happening internally.

Same with emotions, but instead of prescribing medicines that rarely cure, as we do with most chronic illnesses, we have to get to the root cause so we can live a fulfilled and happy life. The "I don't know why I feel this way" can't be the standard any longer. There are always reasons why we feel the way we do, and it is our responsibility to get to that reason.

Why? Because we are 100 percent responsible for our own happiness in life, and if we want to be HOT—which, duh!—then we need to start becoming masters of our emotions. When we become masters of our emotions, we become masters of our life, and when we become masters of our life, we not only attract people who are masters of their own lives, but we are also able to open up and sustain any beautiful relationship.

Side note: If you want to go deeper in the "feelings as teachers," I encourage you to look up Danielle LaPorte's *The Desire Map*. She is absolutely brilliant at getting people connected to their most desired feelings. Life changer!

Seven

The Real Truth About Happiness

Okay! It's about time to get into the truth of truths about this word *happiness*. I've been throwing it around once or twice throughout this book, but we haven't really gotten into what it actually means. No, I'm not talking about the definition (we all know that). I am talking about the reason why so many of us have this word controlling our lives without actually feeling it or living it.

I have heard so many people say they "just want to be happy" as if it's the be-all and end-all. Don't get me wrong. I am fully aware of the title of this book and understand the true power happiness has on the quality of our life, but what if (for shits and giggles) we took happiness out of the equation? What word would you replace it with?

We talked about negative feelings in the previous chapter. There are many descriptions for the way we might feel "bad." After all, the word *bad* is just a word used to generalize an accumulation of shitty feelings, right? If you couldn't say the word *bad*, you would be left having to be very descriptive for the way you feel, which is way better. What if I told you it was the same with the word *happiness*? Happiness is just a word that is a generalization of all the positive emotions we may feel, but there's a problem with that. If we don't know all the specific feelings it takes for us to feel "happy," then "happiness" will be much harder to achieve.

Is your mind twisted yet? Mine is. But here's what I'd like you to understand: We have to start being more descriptive of the way we feel, so that we know what lights us up and how we can sustain happiness long term. Happiness is not an end goal. It is something to be *now,* but we won't know how to get there if we don't get specific with the small things.

Why do I say small things? Because so many times we attach happiness to a rule—a rule we've made up that will make us deserving. I will be happy when I lose X amount of weight (rule). I will be happy when I get promoted to (this) position. I will be happy when I can afford (a particular) house. I will be happy when my husband, boyfriend or girlfriend acts (this) way with me. We make so many rules and conditions to be happy instead of tapping into the small feelings that sustain our happiness right now.

What does that mean? Think about a particular time in your day that makes you feel good. Maybe it's coming home from work, putting your favorite sweats on and having a glass of wine. That feels good, right? Yes. But how would you describe that type of feeling? What would you call that specifically? Would it be comfortable? Cozy? Peaceful? Relieved? Get clear on the small points of happiness throughout your day so you will know how to recreate them. I'm not saying that having a glass of wine is something you should always turn to, but there is something in a glass of wine that we can even dissect. What feeling does it give you that you can recreate throughout your day?

We have many feelings we are attracted to that aid our overall happiness, but if we don't know the feelings we value, we might believe that happiness is for people who have (X, Y, Z) and is not really in the cards for us.

As a young girl, even in midst of the hardships with my mom, I remember that some of my happiest times were when we watched movies together. When my mom, my sister and I would pick out a movie and watch it with all three of us cuddled in bed, I felt like the happiest girl. Sure, I knew it was only for that hour or so, but to me, that was enough. Why? Because, in those hours, I felt safe, comforted and loved. In those hours, we were disconnected from the hardships of life and were in a place of peace. That was the word: peace. As long as we were watching that movie, my life was at peace.

Dissecting that memory was crucial because it helped me understand one of the feelings I honor so much: peace. But that's not the only feeling I honor, and it can't be, because as much as the word *peace* is beautiful, the truth is, it is not realistic to feel peace all the time, right? So let me tell you a different time I was blissfully happy.

When I was younger, my dad would take me everywhere with him. He'd call me his "road dog" and I was the luckiest girl in the world to have a partner in crime like him.

"Moments that make life worth living are when things are at their worst, and you find a way to laugh."

-Amy Schumer

I remember being in the passenger seat of his car, with the music never below the bumping of the bass, while singing our lungs out, accompanied by the most obnoxious chair dances anyone at a stoplight had ever seen in his life (sorry not sorry). Every song gave us an opportunity to showcase our many talents (of which we thought we had). One minute we were the most soulful R&B singer, the next we were challenging Andre 3000 to a rap battle. We'd obviously lose … but the feeling I had on our car rides made me believe I was the happiest girl on earth, and to this day, there's no doubt in my mind that I actually was in those moments, but why? What was the root feeling that made me feel that way?

In dissecting that memory, I came up with three root feelings: playful, authentic and safe. Those moments in my dad's car allowed me to be playful, which my soul needed, especially since I had to be "adult" most of the time at my mom's house. Being playful allowed me to tap into the true essence of my spirit, and for those moments, I was my most authentic self. But the most important feeling I remember was feeling safe enough to be my true self. My dad created a safe space for my spirit to be free, and that allowed me to feel even more connected and loved by him.

Happiness is a universal word, but what determines the happiness of each individual is completely different and may not be what you think it is. Happiness is made up of sub-feelings that you may not have realized. And those feelings may actually be more valuable than "happiness." When I dissected each memory, I also dissected the moments I felt made me happy, but the real feeling of happiness came from sub-feelings, like peace, playfulness, authenticity, safety and connection. But there are so many more feelings that are important to me. They are sort of like my needs.

Motivational speaker Tony Robbins talks of the "six human needs" (which I love), and the list goes a little like this:

- Significance
- Variety
- Certainty
- Love/connection
- Growth
- Contribution

The core of everything that every human being does is to achieve these six needs. We all achieve these needs in different ways, but achieve them we do.

Tony uses a drastic example of Hitler and Mother Teresa sharing the same need for "significance," obviously in completely different ways. Mother Teresa felt significant by knowing she was helping those in need, and Hitler felt significant by ... well ... we know how. Not positive on his side, but every human has the same needs.

Understanding this has helped me become clearer about some of the behaviors and patterns I had become attached to while fulfilling these needs, and some of them, let me tell you, were not good. But, as much as I love Tony Robbins (trust me, I do, as you'll see in my work), I am a feelings type of girl. Always have been and always will be.

At an early age I started realizing just how much I did things to achieve a certain feeling. Now, referencing Tony again, he says that if any one thing you do allows you to achieve *two* of these six human needs, it will become a pattern or an addiction. Again, good or bad.

Let's take an addiction we are seeing going cray cray in this day and age: social media! Most of us here are going to have to raise our hands ... I mean, I see you on Instagram, Facebook, Twitter and now my new obsession, Snapchat. But is there such a thing as social media addiction? Yes!

How many days do you wake up and the first thing you do is check all notifications across all platforms? This is not the time to lie, and so I'll fess up too. But the truth is, the reason we become addicted to social media is because we achieve two or more of our six human needs. We feel *significant* when posting about our life, drama or business. We feel *variety*, because there's something different to read, see or like all the time. We certainly feel *connection* because, well, that's what social media does. More than two of our needs are being met ... and we are addicted.

Now, you may argue that a social media addiction isn't as drastic as drugs, alcohol or smoking. Yes, it may not have a drastic physical effect, but it can have devastating effects on relationships.

But what does this all have to do with happiness? Well, again, I'm a feelings type of girl, and although I am using the six human needs as an example, I believe that dissecting these needs further really comes down to feelings.

What feeling are you ultimately trying to achieve when you reach for that smoke? What feeling are you ultimately trying to achieve when you reach for that drink? What feeling are you ultimately trying to achieve by rushing into a new relationship after a previous one? What feeling are you ultimately trying to achieve when you are reaching for that cookie or brownie? What feeling are you ultimately trying to achieve when you post a picture on social media? What feeling are you ultimately trying to achieve when you buy a new pair of shoes? What feeling are you ultimately trying to achieve when you binge watch your favorite reality TV show?

Something I've noticed is that the feelings we ultimately try to achieve are never negative. They are actually very positive, but the ways in which we try to achieve these feelings might not be so positive.

When I think back to the times I've felt most happy, I see that the sub-feelings that made me feel happy are the same feelings I still value now. (Whew! That was a whole lotta feelings in that sentence.) The feelings I valued never changed, but when I was unhappy I tried to achieve those feelings in negative ways, or ways that weren't congruent to my truth. Let me tell you what I mean.

Let's take one of my most valued feelings, which is connection. Years back, after finally breaking up with a boyfriend with whom I had an on-and-off relationship for four years, I was left learning how to be single. I thought I was doing pretty well, but that couldn't have been further from the truth. I desperately wanted to feel connected, but instead of finding ways to adapt to my new single life and connect to a deeper part of myself, I found every way to achieve connection by drinking excessively, going out way too much and hanging out with people who were fun but didn't really support or align with my truth. Hell, I was so far gone from my truth, so how could they?

Thank goodness I had a couple of solid people in my life, one of whom is my very best friend to this day. Boyyyy, she has seen me at my absolute worst! But to continue the story, I was constantly doing things to achieve the feelings I valued most but in ways that contradicted my truth (who I really was). This contradiction kept me seeking, and the seeking kept me saying "yes" to things that ultimately fucked me over. Remember we talked about saying too many "yeses"?

I became a "yes" machine because I was so uncertain of myself. I started to date guys I knew were beyond wrong for me, but I made up a glamorized image of who they were and why I needed them.

What?! That sounds pathetic now, right? And if I said this out loud I would've probably stopped that shit sooner, but this is the kind of stuff that happens internally, and it's pretty messed up. Did I feel fun and connected when I was going out? Yes. Did I feel good enough when I was picking up the tab (when really I had no money)? Yes. Did I feel at peace when I was drinking excessively? Yes, because it made me block out the hard truth that was yelling at me to get my shit together.

See, good feelings but shitty ways to fulfill them, and we do this without knowing we are. And this, my friend, is the type of stuff that's leaving us feeling unhappy most of the time. Keeping us believing that happiness is outside of ourselves and we aren't worthy of feeling it, when in reality, we have the power to feel good at any time. We just need to bring awareness to it, and that's just what we are going to do.

DISSECT YOUR MEMORIES

1. I want you to think of a time that brought you pure joy, something that made you light up and in that moment you felt happy.

2. Now, dissect that memory. What was the sub-feeling(s) that was underlying your happiness in that moment? Remember, watching movies with my mom I felt connected and at peace, and during the car rides with my dad I felt playful, authentic, connected, loved and safe. In the dissection you will realize the feelings you value most. Danielle LaPorte calls them "core desired feelings." God, I love her!

3. Write these feelings down and make sure you become aware of them!

4. Now, how did/do you dishonor these feelings? Like I said in my story, throughout my life I was always achieving these feelings, but at certain stages I was achieving them in negative ways. So take a moment and write down how you are currently trying to achieve these feelings that may not be serving you or the sustainability of your happiness.

5. Now examine how you could (or do) honor these feelings. How do/can you achieve these feelings in positive ways? For example, I feel connected when I express my love to those I care about. I feel connected when I am able to talk about my day with Andrew. I feel connected after a good workout at the gym.

6. Start creating your list of ways you honor your feelings. Hint: You will see that the ways you honor your feelings are the ways you honor your values.

THE REAL TRUTH AND NOTHING BUT THE TRUTH

Happiness is a feeling. And feelings are fleeting. Oops, what? "How could she say that but write a book on how to be happy?"

Yes, I know. Let me finish. The happiness we are taught to seek is fleeting. The happiness we are able to sustain in life is an accumulation of the feelings we honor most. That is what happiness is and why happiness is unique to every person.

So before you start attaching happiness to a goal, situation or stage of life, you have to understand that none—I repeat, none—of those things will bring you happiness. Catering to the feelings you want to feel in the ways that make your spirit most alive is where happiness lives.

The more we understand this, the more fulfilling our relationships will become, first with ourselves and then with others.

With that said, here are four ways to feel your version of happiness. Again, your happiness is different from mine, but the practice is the same.

What have you laughed about today?

If the answer is nothing, you better get to it! Laughter is your cheapest medicine.

The Practice: Sustainable Happiness

1. Get present: In order to feel happy now you need to be in the "now." Sounds simple, but it is so hard for us to do. We are constantly thinking of what we need to achieve in the future, or worse, we live in our past stories. We are hardly ever in the moment, because if we were, we would see more of the miracles that surround us, which would bring us closer to the feelings we want to feel! Which brings me to the next step ...

2. Get clear on what you want to feel: Like I said before, happiness is just a feeling, but we all have different ways of feeling happy. We don't even have to use the word *happy* if we don't want to. There are tons of different ways to describe this feeling. Here are a few, just to give you an idea. I definitely encourage you to create a list of your own!

Do you like to feel authentic, energetic, empowered, playful, sexy, feminine, loved, healthy, inspired, vibrant, whole, peaceful or openhearted? Go on, you can create your own list. I know we did a mini version of this earlier, but create an elaborate list and circle the ones that are really important for you to feel.

3. Write down how you can achieve that feeling: The next step is to write under each of your favorite feelings *how* can you achieve it, starting now. What makes you feel vibrant? What makes you feel sexy? What makes you feel you are at peace? The truth is, these wouldn't be your favorite feelings if you hadn't felt them before, so you already know how to access them. You just need to be able to remember that feeling so you can access it every day.

4. Practice gratitude: Sounds cliché, right? But it's so necessary! Ladies, if you are reading this book, then you have a strong drive to create goodness in your life! How amazing is that? If you are reading this, I know you have a shit ton of things to be grateful for. I mean, what about all the people in your life who have brought you here to this point? All the experiences in your life that have made you stronger? The love inside of you that sees more for yourself and wants you to grow? What about your family, pets, significant others, friends?

Here's the thing: it's easy to say we are thankful for these, but I want you to go deeper. If you have a journal (if not, get one), write a list of things you are grateful for. Again, these can be people, experiences (good or bad), things you own that you've worked hard to get, even resources ... anything. Just write them down.

Then I want you to go even deeper. Below each thing you are grateful for, write why it is so significant in your life. For example, if you wrote that you are grateful for your home, what does your home do for you? How does your home make you feel? How many people has your home hosted and also made feel good?

Spend as long as you can to create these lists, because the truth is that happiness is a feeling that can be accessed at any time. Passion is a feeling that can be accessed any time. Love is a feeling that can be accessed any time. Wealth is a feeling that can be accessed any time. The more we access these feelings, the more amplified they will become!

APPS TO LIVE BY

While we are on the gratitude train, I want to mention two apps that I absolutely adore. They are good for anyone who is constantly on the go but understands the power of gratitude and meditation.

Headspace: This app will guide you through a ten-minute meditation. If you don't have ten minutes to give yourself, then you really are in trouble.

Gratitude: This app will send a cute alert at a specific time throughout the day, so you can log what you are thankful for. The more you start getting into a gratitude practice, the more you will notice all the abundance that surrounds you.

Take the time to download them now!

Your problem wasn't because you *listened* to your heart, it's because you *didn't*.

Eight

Ways You Could Be F***ing Up a Relationship

By this chapter, I'm gonna say, we are used to getting real with ourselves, and that's a good thing, because this topic is going to need a lot of realness. But we're all about the real life, though, so I think you are ready!

As we know, relationships are a bit complicated at times, just as life is. I mean, relationships are life and as I've said before, life is all about relating and connecting, not only to ourselves but also to other people and other things.

The complicated part of relationships comes from the fact that we can't always control the good or bad that comes with them. Sometimes we meet the wrong people. Sometimes the most passionate loves fade. Sometimes people change and are no longer conducive to our growth. Sometimes we do well financially and sometimes we don't. Sometimes we are on track with our health and other times we aren't, because life gets in the way. Sometimes we feel fully connected to our truth and other times we feel scatterbrained with all of life's "to-dos."

Things happen, and relationships are constantly changing with or without our permission. But what about the times our relationships take a turn for the worse because of some things we do without even realizing it? Sure, it's so easy to blame outside circumstances and other people for the demise, disruption or end of a relationship. It is also easy to get caught up in what's not working for us instead of acknowledging and becoming aware of what is.

Throughout the years I've had ladies come to me with different issues, anything from not feeling loved by their significant other, to not being rewarded for their hard work, to not being able to stick to a health regimen for very long. Through all these women, I noticed something phenomenal; I noticed that in every disruption we believe is happening in our lives, there is a certain energy that we emit with it.

There is a certain essence of being that many of us have that more than likely existed even before the disrupted relationship happened. We like to believe our attitude and restricted energy are because of what's going on, when that's just not true. I guess, without beating around the bush, what I am saying is, we are fucking up our own relationships without even knowing we are, and it is through a combination of these five things:

1. Bringing negative energy into your space

2. Looking for bad intentions in people

3. Making stuff up

4. Putting yourself down

5. Doing things for the wrong reasons

It is these things that I have dissected and have seen to be at the core of many of the disruptions in our lives. Let's look at each one.

1. BRINGING NEGATIVE ENERGY INTO YOUR SPACE

Take note: This is *muy importante*.

"Please take responsibility for the energy you bring into this space."

This quotation was said by Dr. Jill Bolte Taylor in her TED Talk called "My Stroke of Insight."

I will forever re-quote this, because to me life is all about energy. After all, we are walking, talking, breathing balls of energy. But what we don't realize is just how powerful our energy is and how much damage we cause by allowing negative energy to reside in and around us.

How many times have you been able to pick up on someone's energy to the extent that it actually made you feel a certain way? Whether it felt good or bad, we all have, right?

Even without speaking, we all have the gift to pick up on each other's energy. For feminine energy (I will not say "women" because feminine and masculine energies are not specific to genders) this gift is even more powerful, because feminine energy is about intuition. Feminine energy thinks for a community. It tends to feel more of what's happening around it. Like nature, it is in a constant state of flow and adaptability, and the reason why it is able to flow like this is because it is constantly connecting with other energies.

Don't be in a relationship because you feel it will validate who you are. Be in a relationship because *you know what you can give.*

Insecurities come from a lack of love flowing within. When there's a lack of love flowing within, there will always be a lack of love flowing in your relationships.

This is not to say that masculine energy doesn't do these things, but it is just completely different energetically and is powerful in other ways. What we must know is that we all embody both energies at different times, but if we aren't careful, we can fall out of balance and embody one energy that may not be congruent to our being. This will leave us feeling unhappy, unsatisfied, disconnected and in "seeking" mode.

Oh yeah, how you live energetically is a big fucking deal! How? Something I see very often is a woman (who is truly feminine to the core) embodying more of her masculine side, which could happen for many reasons, but what she doesn't know is this behavior greatly affects her happiness and is one of the most common reasons she doesn't feel connected. Some of the reasons for us embodying an energy that's not true to us could be due to the following:

It Is Something We Were Taught or Felt Obligated to Be to Feel Loved

Take a moment and look back to a time you felt most loved by the people you care about. Sometimes the ladies I find living more in their masculinity remember a time where in order to feel most loved by certain family members (i.e., fathers, uncles, grandparents, brothers, cousins, friends) they had to do things that connected more to their masculine side. This is especially true for the people they really looked up to or admired. What happens is we become attached to the ways that have been successful in achieving love. We may even find we grew so attached to these ways of achieving love that they become a part of "who we are," making it hard to let go of these attachments, even when they are no longer serving us. Yes, that is something I hear so much: "That's just who I am ..." But as we've learned throughout this book, who we are is not determined by the made-up beliefs about "how it should be," especially if we don't really know how it should be because it's not making us happy.

Societal Pressures of "How It Should Be"

In this day and age, women (especially in our generation) are able to do all they want and more, whether it is professionally, personally or financially, and it is beautiful to see! My ladies are doing it all, but with that comes a crazy phenomena, which is the pressure we create within ourselves to do it all.

We are taking on so many roles from a place of merely proving ourselves that we are becoming more and more disconnected to how we want to feel. We are learning that in order to be a "successful" woman, we have to compromise the most beautiful parts of our femininity. We are learning to adopt an attitude of independence in order to prove we are worthy enough. This can conflict with the feminine power, which comes from the ability to connect and feel.

We are suppressing the very feminine qualities of ourselves, believing they are weak and unnecessary. It's crazy! I was once at brunch with a lady who was absolutely golden "on paper." If there were anyone you thought had it all together, it would be her. There was so much I respected about her, and still do, because she was just so driven and clear about her vision professionally. She has even inspired tons of women to start their own businesses and create a life of their choosing. Beautiful, right?

Well, the truth was, she wasn't fulfilled nor happy. She found temporary joy in her work and achievements, but when it came to personal passion, there was nothing. She had been in and out of failed relationships, most of which ended by her saying, "We just grew apart."

What I noticed with her story and so many others is that we rarely reflect on what actually fell apart. We rarely see the small parts of the relationship that were the most critical. And what I've realized is, the energy that you bring and embody within yourself could be the most critical part to any sustainable relationship.

Here's what I mean. I like to ask women what they think they are. I simply ask, "Do you think you're masculine or feminine?" And the majority of the responses I get, even from women who are very feminine, is "Oh! I know I'm masculine." But they say it in a tone that feels proud of it. Again, nothing is wrong with either energy—they are both powerful as hell—but we need to make sure we are embodying the right one for our spirit.

But what I am finding is that women prefer to identify as masculine because at some core level, we think that feminine is weak … seriously?! I see this even with ladies who identify as "feminists"! How can we believe the feminine energy is weak yet live a life empowering the "feminine"? That's a contradiction to me if I've ever heard one. A contradiction that inflicts more harm internally because we are not being true to who we are.

Again, femininity is not gender based. There are men who are naturally feminine. There are women who are naturally masculine. And every person has both energies. But we need to connect with our most natural energy and learn how to come back to that. Not only for ourselves, but for our relationships as well. It's time for us to stop the subconscious dialogue that says the feminine energy is weak because this is what's causing most of us to feel passionless and unconnected. Why? Because we are pretending to be something we are not.

Going back to the discussion with the lady at brunch, because I wanted to get to the bottom of her relationship issue, I asked her what kind of men she liked. She said, "One hundred percent masculine men."

Relationships are very delicate and precious, and without the right care, can be easily damaged.

The ability to RECEIVE love is just as powerful as GIVING it.

Here's how our conversation went down:

Me: "You identify as a masculine yet want a masculine man?"

Her: [Laughs.]

Me: "A true masculine is attracted to the feminine. [Notice I did not mention gender.] It is the polarity of the energies that creates passion and allows relationships to flow. My guess is, in the beginning of your relationships, you were able to embody your feminine, which was how and why they were attracted to you in the first place and how you were attracted to them, but over time, because you were so used to using your masculine energy more due to the roles you've had to play in your life (which I'm not belittling), there was a shift in your relationships. The shift that, before this, you described as 'we just grew apart.'"

Her: [At a loss for words] "I'm just so used to being in control."

Me: "Yes, professionally—which is great! But when you come home with masculine energy to a *masculine* man, he will do one of two things: He will turn feminine (even if he's not feminine naturally) because he loves you and wants to keep the peace. Or, he will leave if he chooses his masculinity more because the attraction is gone."

Her: "The first one would usually happen: I became unattracted because I felt he had changed. Now that makes sense why it seemed that way."

She realized that she flipped the script in most of her relationships. Up until now she had never understood why her relationships would always fail, which just created a negative belief about relationships, about men and even about herself. The energy she used in business was not conducive for the relationship she wanted intimately. Again (I can't say it enough), we all have both energies; we just need to know which one we must live in most of the time to be congruent with ourselves.

This type of conversation didn't just happen with her; it is at the core of every problem I help women with, especially if they are struggling with feeling connection and passion. Here, I only shared an example of how not embodying our natural energies affects our intimate relationships, but it really affects our total lives.

Do you want to know what living your truth means? It means you are embodying your most natural energy. The energy of your soul. Only when we are able to do that can we truly radiate beautiful energy around us. When we live incongruent to our natural energy, we slowly destroy our spirit, and this destroys the relationships around us by bringing negative and restricted energy into our space. We will talk more about how to right this in the upcoming chapters!

(This was the longest step, I promise!)

2. LOOKING FOR BAD INTENTIONS IN PEOPLE

This one is huge! Have you ever been with someone who always questioned you about everything you did that you felt you had to explain yourself all the time? How did that feel? Not good, right?

We talked about this a little in Chapter 3 when we discussed victimizing patterns. However, this is a little different. This isn't necessarily about becoming victimized by a person; this just comes straight from a pessimistic way of viewing the world, and it serves no purpose if you are trying to live a fulfilling life.

This behavior will leave you believing every person has an ulterior motive and being skeptical of most people and even opportunities that seem too good to be true. No, I don't believe we should float around like little fairies with our head in the clouds, thinking everything is a bed of roses (although that would be more fun), but I do believe we need to stop actively searching for the bad intentions in people, unless you don't mind destroying the relationships you have around you.

I see this a lot with couples, where we (yes, I said "we," because I even fall into this pattern at times) tend to get mad over small things because we made up in our heads that our partners "intentionally" did something to us. Intentionally didn't listen. Intentionally didn't put his/her dishes away. Intentionally didn't respond to my text message. Intentionally left his socks on the floor.

Remember what we discussed before about taking things personally? Well, looking for bad intentions in those around us makes everything personal. The more we take personally, the more we separate ourselves from true connection and severely damage the relationship we are in.

If we can look at the greater intentions of people, especially our spouses, family, friends, coworkers and so on, we will be able to come from a place of understanding.

3. MAKING STUFF UP

Making things up could be a beautiful and creative trait if you are in the arts, but it definitely doesn't work in relationships, especially if your made-up reality is one that is disempowering to you or your relationships. Do you catch yourself saying something close to the following:

"There aren't any good guys out there."

"My husband didn't hug me when he came in ... I think we are becoming distant ... Is he seeing someone else?"

"Suzy didn't help me at work today. She doesn't care about anyone but herself."

As soon as you think you are not enough, you start behaving in ways that aren't enough for your *true self*.

All thoughts create stories, which turn into feelings that turn into negative or positive energy. So we want to make sure our thoughts aren't coming from a disempowering place. As I said before, energy is fuel that creates passion in our relationships. One of the ways we destroy this passion is by making up disempowering stories.

4. PUTTING YOURSELF DOWN

When you don't feel enough, you will act in ways that are not enough for your true self.

It takes two full people to have a successful relationship, and when one is in self-pity mode, it makes it harder for the other person. Why? Because no one can compensate for the lack of fulfillment within.

Your thoughts become the energy you bring (you've got that by now, right?). When there is a lack of love flowing internally, there will always be a lack of love flowing externally, which is not sustainable for a healthy relationship.

There was a time in my relationship when I felt I wasn't good enough. It was when I first started my business. I always felt inadequate and started to question myself daily. If there were a microphone for the things I'd say about myself to myself … let's just say thank goodness there wasn't.

Starting The Ladies Coach pushed out my deep insecurities, which came from not feeling smart enough or savvy enough to actually start something because I saw so many people doing it better than me. Even writing this book I had to overcome feelings of inadequacy, but the difference now is I have the tools (which we discussed in Chapter 6) to check myself when these feelings happen. It's so good to be able to check yourself when feelings of inadequacy arise because I came to realize that the insecure moments I had at the beginning of my business trickled into other aspects of my life. It was no longer something I made up internally, because those thoughts turned into my energy, and that energy affected my relationship.

Thankfully, Andrew is a very patient and understanding man and knew what was going on even when I didn't, but it still put a damper on our connection. Good men just want to make you happy, and when they see you suffering internally, they feel like a failure. It's okay to have temporary times when we are uncertain about ourselves, but going through long periods of self-pity will make any relationship hard to sustain. We are responsible for our own happiness.

5. DOING THINGS FOR THE WRONG REASONS

Here are some questions to think about:

- Are you always finding ways to please people that sometimes it leaves you drained with no time for yourself?

- Are you a successful lady who has worked your ass off to get to where you are, but still feel there is a lack of passion?

- Are you someone who is in a relationship because you feel being with anyone is better than being alone?

- Are you in business because you want to prove yourself or live up to someone's expectation of you?

Personally, I used to be a people pleaser to the extreme. In some weird way, I thought "pleasing" people was "helping" people, which holds some truth, especially since my passion is to "help" people. But the *real* truth wasn't that pretty. The truth was, I desperately wanted to feel good enough! I loved hearing that praise/recognition, and I certainly got a lot out of it, but that "feel-good feeling" was very temporary.

I was constantly out of energy and felt I needed to keep giving my time and energy away in order to feel good enough; it was almost like an addiction. I quickly realized I was pleasing people for the wrong reasons. The discovery part is also the powerful part (if you do something with it). Since that discovery, I slowly started setting more and more boundaries and allowed myself permission to live for me.

We have all been guilty of some, if not all, of these crimes, but it's not about being right or wrong—it's about growing from it in a way that encourages love. And if you can do this, you will be on a solid path to powerful and passionate relationships, starting with the most important relationship: yourself!

Nine

Get Turned On!
What Do You Really Want?

I don't know about you, but I think the most beautiful thing to see is a women so unbelievably filled up and turned on. Not just turned on sexually, which is always hot, but I'm talking about being turned on to life. Waking up excited for what she can create around her. Creativity lives in us all and is expressed in different forms, but I hear so many women believe that they aren't creative. This couldn't be further from the truth.

Most of us believe that creativity lives primarily in those talented in the "arts," but really to be creative means you look outside the box. It means you are imaginative, resourceful, experimental, innovative and inspired. I've always loved the word *inspired* because to be inspired you have to be "in spirit," and to be in spirit means you are *turned on*. You are turned on to the way things "can be" instead of the way things "have to be." And the truth is, there is nothing that kills creativity more than believing life is one way. Creativity, in its essence, is truly about believing there are multiple ways of living.

Since this book is about being HOT, and we've already talked a great deal about what it means to be happy ("H"), let's get on with "O," which means to be open. Openness is about courage. Courage to step into all that you are and feeling shameless in the process. But so very often, women I speak to can't help but feel guilty about doing things that make them light up and, in turn, they suppress their deepest desires. I don't know about you, but can anyone else see the danger in doing that?

Suppression causes aggression.

It's true! So often I see women suppressing their own expansive light, and when we do that, we become aggressive toward others, especially to fellow women. We've seen this, right? We see it online in comment sections. We see it in the workplace. We see it in grocery stores. We see it within our families and we also see it in the media.

Suppressing our spirit is not only emotionally and socially damaging but physically damaging as well. Our physical body is tied to our energy, and when we restrict our energy, our health gets compromised. Let me ask you, when you get anxious, stressed or depressed, do you ever notice what your body does? It caves in! Your shoulders and back may slump, your head lowers and your breasts cave in. Most important, what happens to your breathing? Our breath becomes super shallow, which suppresses the oxygen necessary for our cells to carry to our vital organs, which causes even more physical issues.

Everything is so related, hence the reason I believe relationships are so powerful. Relationships, to me, are the understanding that everything is connected. You can't look at one thing without looking at *everything*. I have so many people ask me what is my one tip for happiness, or one tip for success, or one tip for healthy relationships. As you may have realized by now, there is no one tip. Every human being is different, and we are always going to be at different stages in our life, but if there were to be just one tip for happiness, I would say that it is dependent on one thing—and that is you and how turned on you are with life. When you are turned on, your energy is expansive and you are less apt to get sucked in by emotional roller coasters.

One talk I especially love is by the well-known author of *Eat, Pray, Love*, Elizabeth Gilbert. She spoke at an event by Oprah and the focus of her talk was on "finding your passion." (That wasn't the name of her talk, just the theme.)

For Elizabeth Gilbert, finding her passion was not something she had to do. From an early age, she knew writing was "it" for her. It was her expression of creativity and the art of her soul. There was no "finding passion" for her, as it was pretty clear. Like many people in my field, she would often go around giving talks about "finding your passion," like it's this one thing in you, gifted to you, and that it's your job to dissect what that is and live it!

In many ways that is true, but what felt so relieving in her most recent talk was that she made an apology for that type of belief. She told the audience that not everyone has that one thing, and that's okay. Some people have multiple things that interest them, and dissecting their multiple interests would be completely restricting.

"A woman in harmony with her spirit is like a river flowing. She goes where she will without pretense and arrives at her destination prepared to be herself and only herself."

-Maya Angelou

"It's not the imbalances of life that will get you down—it's doing meaningless things that aren't taking you where you want to go."

−Danielle LaPorte

I couldn't agree more with her discovery, and I honor her for that realization, among many other things about her.

How many times have you looked to other people who seem to have their "thing" and think, "Why don't I have my 'thing' yet?" Personally, I've always felt I was interested in so many things that I almost got jealous when people found their one passion. It made me feel insecure about mine, actually. I mean, why can't I be focused on one particular thing for very long?

Take my hubby, for example. Andrew is a professional poker player, and he knew at a young age that he wanted to play poker. Still to this day he gets excited to play and is one of the hardest working people I know because he is so passionate about what he does.

I am completely different. I don't have one singular passion. I am multi-passionate and it took me a very long time to accept that as okay.

I now prefer what Elizabeth Gilbert says: "Follow your curiosity." What I have realized is the more interests we explore, the more things start to make sense, and who knows? It might lead you to a singular passion or multiple passions. But there's one thing we have to understand. Like happiness, passion is just a feeling. A feeling that gives us purpose and excitement. A feeling (like other feelings) we can choose to feel every day.

How does passion relate to openness? Creativity, passion and purpose are all about being open. Being open feels so good to the soul. Openness is where authenticity and expression live, and the more we discover what allows us to feel open and expressive, the more we are able to live in our natural energy. And remember we talked about how your natural energy is important to sustaining your relationships? Yup! It all connects! So before we get into the discovery mode, let's prep ourselves a bit.

LET'S GET PHYSICAL

You can't think yourself into passion and creativity. There will be times when we get into downright shitty moods, and no matter how hard we try to think positively, it just doesn't work. But that's where we get it wrong in the first place. *Thinking* doesn't get us turned on ... *moving* and *doing* do! You have to move! I love a quote that's been floating around social media that says, "Drink some coffee, put on some gangsta rap and handle it." Yes!

Get yourself moving. When you start moving, it will lead you to more things than if you just sat around "thinking." When I go through patches of feeling uninspired, I put on some music and move! Moving allows your energy to start flowing, and when your energy is flowing, good things start to happen.

When your body is restricted, your energy is restricted. When your energy is restricted, your love is restricted. When your love is restricted, you will allow shitty relationships and shitty circumstances around you. So get your buns up and start moving! Whatever that may be to you, just move your body.

LAUGH

Yes, laughing is a universal pleasure, and the practice of laughter releases so many emotions. There is something so vulnerable and open about laughter because there is no hiding from something your spirit finds funny. I learn so much about myself through laughter because laughter comes from the truest parts of me. I can't hold back laughter; if it wants to come out, it comes out. What you find funny could be a small connection to something bigger, and not only that, but laughter is the most natural medicine there is. I'm sure you heard that before, but here's the reason why: laughter releases endorphins, the chemicals that make you feel good temporarily because it relieves pain. While endorphins are floating around, there's really no way to let stress, anxiety and depression get you down—at least for those moments, right? But even if we are talking about minutes of bliss, if we are really able to not feel negative emotions temporarily and from our own doing, then couldn't there be a more sustainable way of feeling happiness? Let's not overwhelm ourselves now; just know that the more we find things to laugh at, the less serious we take life and the more movement and flow we allow, the more we will be able to adapt to even the hardest of times. Not to mention, laughter is you turned on!

ALLOW YOURSELF THE FREEDOM TO EXPLORE

Here's where openness takes courage. Exploring takes you out of your comfort zone, and that's what needs to happen in order for your spirit to grow and for you to stop feeling stuck. There's so many times I will talk to ladies, and when they are asked, "What do you like to do?" or "What are some things you do that make you feel good?" they respond with the famous "I don't know."

It is definitely okay not to know, but it is not okay to stay there. We are responsible for our own joy and happiness, yet too many of us are waiting for outside things to turn the spark on inside of us. We can't wait anymore; we have to start exploring. The more we try new things, or even the old things we knew once brought us joy, the more control we start taking over our ability to shift our world.

The Practice: "Turn It On"

First, allow at least ten minutes for just you and this practice. If you are reading this now, then it's safe to say this would be the best time for you to do this practice.

Clear your space of any distractions. Put some soft music on, maybe light a candle or two and get yourself in a place where you feel most expressive.

Move your body around a little bit. Do a few jumps or stretches, dance or even meditate! Do something that is going to get you out of your head and into your body. (I personally think dancing is the best way for me to get into my body and out of my head.)

Hint: Getting out of your head is necessary for this practice because your head is often what keeps you feeling stuck and, worse, we begin to judge ourselves. The more we are in our bodies, the more we are able to reflect from a place of truth.

1. Get a paper and pen (unless you are a tech geek, then open up a blank document on your computer or phone and get ready).

2. Without looking at your blank screen or paper (yes, I said without looking: it's okay if it comes out scribbled), start writing/typing all the things you've been wanting to try but never made the time for. It could be anything as small as giving yourself five minutes of silence a day (that might be something huge for the mommies out there) to maybe trying a wine-tasting or an art class! Again, whatever comes through, write it down. Spend a good five minutes of writing.

Hint: The reason I say "without looking" is because it's so easy for us to judge what we write or second guess it because too much logical thinking will get in the way.

3. After the five minutes are up, circle three of the items on your list and rewrite these three on a new piece of paper. Again, if you are a techy, cut and paste those three items into a new document.

4. Now, get your calendar out! This is where we all turn techies, because we all know the only calendar we use is on our phones. Don't even make the excuse that you don't have one because we all know that's a lie! You are going to schedule the items you circled into your calendar.

Is it in your calendar? Good.

Here comes the hard part …

5. Once these things go into your calendar, they become non-negotiables. What are non-negotiables? Well, they are things you cannot negotiate or change. They are must-dos, no matter what. The non-negotiable practice is *very* important. The reason I see so many women unhappy is because we are saying "yes" to everything else besides our own wants and needs. Non-negotiables pretty much say the "no" for you. It's as if you have an important meeting with yourself. In fact, if someone were to ask you for your time, you can very well say, "I have a meeting that day/time." Or, if that sounds too hoity-toity, then you can simply say, "I can't, I'm doing something at that time." What a grand concept, right? But it can be the hardest because, again, we feel everyone and everything else is more deserving of our time than we are. Let's stop that shit because we are giving beyond our own emotional bank accounts when we do this.

In order to truly feel turned on, energetic and vibrant with our own lives we have to stop caving in to the feelings and tasks of others and start making non-negotiables for ourselves. We serve no one if our energy is completely drained. In fact, it is completely damaging to our relationships and our purpose if we are walking around depleted.

Actually, one of the major causes of breakups, divorce or separation in intimate relationships is the lack of energy that is being given between partners, especially when kids are in the mix. I'm a better lover, sister, daughter and friend when I have taken time out for myself to restore my energy. I am absolutely hell to be around (and too many people close to me will attest) when I feel depleted.

Most women believe that if they cater to every need of the people close to them, then they are proving their love, but often we forget that it doesn't matter how much we do for people if we do it with a shitty attitude and depleted energy. Everyone feels your energy, and if you show up restricted, then you contradict everything you are doing for them.

For example, a wife can say, "I do everything for him and he doesn't appreciate any of it." One reason he may not seem to appreciate it is because all he feels is the energy behind it: the lack of love, the increase in expectations and the nagging about what he has done wrong. All human beings want to feel love, and even when we think we are doing all we can to express love, if our energy doesn't reflect it, then it will be hard for our loved ones to feel it; in turn, it will feel like they aren't appreciative.

The more we are able to fill our love bucket up, the more we do things out of pure love and intention for others. The most important thing to living a life "turned on" is not living out of expectations of what others can do for us. Feeling filled up allows us to show up wholeheartedly for others. But we can't do that when we are living in monotony and feeling stuck.

"If you want to know the secrets of the universe, think in terms of energy, frequency and vibration."

-Nikola Tesla

"I find that when I see women who are comfortable in their skin whatever that is, however that is and whatever way that manifests itself. It's beautiful!"

-Alicia Keys

CREATE A VISION

"It's not the imbalances of life that will get you down, it's doing meaningless things that aren't taking you where you want to go," says Danielle LaPorte.

When you hear the word *vision*, what does it feel like to you? To many, it can mean some huge dream and, at times, may feel overwhelming. The word *vision* definitely used to be overwhelming to me because I felt like I had to keep up or "one up" the visions of others. When I used to hear other people's visions for their lives, I'd hear things like what kind of businesses they wanted to own or how much money they wanted to make, and as great as that is, I never had a dream to make a kazillion dollars or own a business. My vision was always, and still is, to be happy, at peace and in love with my life in whatever way that manifests, but I couldn't say that out loud because I always felt like I wasn't dreaming big enough.

I'd go to seminars with people in my industry and in some way, shape or form, they'd always say "dream big," and when we'd break up into small groups to discuss our "visions," I felt like it was a competition in dreams. Seriously! I'd try to make up some bullshit vision for my business or my life that really didn't feel good only to seem like I was "dreaming big." Why? Because, again, I felt like my dreams just weren't big enough. As hard as I tried to think of specific things that I envisioned for my life, I felt not "creative" enough. Do you ever feel like that?

When someone asks you, "What's your vision for your life?" do you get a little stumped or think your answer might not be exciting enough? These are the kinds of judgments we have about ourselves without even realizing it, and it's crazy, right? Well, I realized that creating a vision that doesn't feel good is worthless. It's like goals: If you have goals that don't really have a strong enough *why*, then, more than likely, you are going to fail that goal or, worse, achieve something that doesn't really feel good. It's kind of like how there are many people with professional success and money who are truly unhappy.

Now, I'm not saying that having a vision isn't necessary. Actually, having a vision for your life is *beyond* necessary—we just have to do it a bit differently (at least for most of us). I realized quickly that my hesitation in vision/goal setting had more to do with my own insecurities than anything else. I thought that what I valued and what was most important for me wouldn't sound good to others. Then I realized that the greatest vision you could ever create for yourself is always about how you want to feel!

When you know how you want to feel, you will do things that promote that feeling every day, instead of creating a specific situation for yourself and hoping it makes you feel a certain way. So why is creating a vision for yourself so important?

Every person needs something to aspire to. It doesn't matter who you are or even how old you are. Every single one of us needs to have something we work toward every day. If we don't have something to aspire to, we will continue to do meaningless and unfulfilling things that slowly eat away at our destiny. (Sounds dramatic, but so true.)

Let's flip the script. How does it feel to be around someone unmotivated, uninspired and completely drained with life? It sucks, right? Unless you don't know because you are that person. (I've certainly been there.) Now, incorporate that feeling into your close relationships. Could you imagine if your spouse continually brought that energy around you? That absolutely *kills* passion, intimacy and attraction. Having a vision for what kind of person you want to be and how you want to leave your footprints on this earth is absolutely crucial if you want to be turned on to life.

There are so many people I idolize for the legacy and imprint they've made in my life. No, they aren't famous, have kazillions of dollars or are creating something to benefit all of humanity. They are people who have recognized the impact they make on their families and have created a vision for how they want to do that. They are constantly growing every day and showing up the best way they can. My grandmother, for instance, is eighty-one years old (Connie, from Mexico) and loves to read every book I've read on my Kindle. She reads them way faster than me and loves to talk about them with me (most of the time I haven't even finished them yet). She will walk circles around all of us and is always doing things that feel good to her. In doing so, she eats quality food, goes out on daily walks to bond with nature and loves to cook for our family. These are the things that light her up, and in turn, her energy is always expansive and impactful.

I have another grandmother (Louise) who is the same in different ways. She is constantly doing things on her own—she even does her own oil changes!—and loves to keep up with everyone, even if it means posting on our Facebook walls more than she should.

My mentors, Joe and Maureen, who are in their seventies, came into my life when I was seventeen years old, while I was working my first job at a casino. Their energy and love are what started our now twelve years (and counting) of friendship. In fact, they are why I am doing what I do. They have taught me the power relationships have in our lives and believe that everyone has a story to tell. And they don't just believe that—they actually walk their talk and spend their days being a part of different organizations and youth groups. They even allow people into their homes for free mentorships. They constantly create a new vision for themselves and how they want to be, which keeps their light shining bright.

So I ask you, no matter where you are in life or how bad circumstances might be at this time, what vision do you have for the type of person you want to be? And how would that person live every day? What would she allow or not allow in her life? What would she give? How would she make others feel? What would she need to know about herself starting now?

In order for us to get turned on, we need to know what kind of woman we want to be and how we want to exist from this day forward. From there, we can determine the things that need to happen daily in order to be that woman. The more we stop doing meaningless things that don't cater to our overall vision and happiness, the better our lives become.

Ten

What Really Is a Good Relationship, Anyway?

It doesn't matter who you are, we all know, intellectually, that it is important to have healthy relationships around us. Most toxic relationships don't happen because we are intellectually searching for them. They happen because we are subconsciously (hidden behind our consciousness) and unconsciously (without awareness) drawn to them. It is important to understand these words because the state of our life happens beyond what we actually see, and it is our job to become more aware. Why? Because it's just not cute anymore to not take responsibility for the state of our relationships.

In the beginning of the book we spoke about values. Our values are the bus driver to our life, and the more we honor them, the more consciously (aware) we live, and that's what we ultimately want. We want to make sure that every aspect of our lives is congruent to our truth because our relationships depend on it. If you don't value yourself, the wrong people will come along and think they don't have to value you either. If we continue to seek validation from others, we will constantly be putting our happiness in other people's hands, only to find we aren't getting what we deserve.

So what is a bad/toxic relationship anyway, and how do we know if we are in one? Can we get a drumroll, please ... A toxic relationship is any relationship based on fear. When you create a relationship or stay in a relationship because you fear a certain outcome, then you are in a toxic environment even if your partner happens to be a good person.

UNDERSTANDING FEAR-BASED EMOTIONS

Fear-based emotions are any emotions driven by fear. Let's dissect fear a little more, shall we? I don't think fear should get a bad rap, which it usually does. Fear actually does serve a purpose if it's controlled. Fear is the alert of danger ahead. It's saved us from close encounters with lions, tigers and bears, "oh my." It stops us from getting too close to the edge of a cliff. It alerts us of an attack, and many more. But here's the thing. We are overworking fear. We've given it way too many jobs. Instead of it being an alert system to immediate dangers, we've allowed it to take control of most aspects of our lives. We've given it so much power that we don't feel empowered enough to make decisions for ourselves.

After all, emotional fear, which is the most damaging kind of fear, makes the assumption that we are not enough and that we need to protect ourselves from ourselves. When we do that, we start seeking: we seek people, food, alcohol, drugs, reality TV, work, social media ... anything for us to feel comforted and safe. The bat shit crazy thing is, we often put ourselves in more harm by listening to fear than if we didn't listen to fear at all. Why? Because there is no abundance that lives through fear. Abundance is a "love-based" emotion and one that comes from the belief that we are more than enough. When we believe we are more than enough, we honor our values, we say no to what doesn't feel right and we let go of the need to play victim.

Oh, how all this is coming together!

Fear-based emotions don't just happen out of nowhere; they are intimately tied to the beliefs and stories we've made up about ourselves and our lives. They are what we've come to know without even being conscious of it. They are mostly born innocently, though. Let me give you an example.

A young girl, raised by a single mother, feels abandoned by her father because he left her and her mother. To protect herself from that pain in the future, she seeks partnership in any relationship with a male, even if it's toxic. Why? Because, to her (her belief) if he's there, she feels loved—even if "being there" comes with unnecessary baggage and toxicity.

Her fear of not "having" is what constantly gets her into relationships that aren't fulfilling because she will always settle for what she believes love looks like, instead of what love feels like. Is this her fault, though? Kinda-sorta-not ... Sure, we only know what we know and how we've dealt with potential threats (fear) in the past, but it's also our responsibility to become more aware, and that starts with valuing who we are and what we have to offer.

Everyone wants a beautiful relationship, but no one wants to put in the work it takes to *keep it.*

Create a love that is safe enough to invite spontaneity; a love that is strong enough for the weak times; a love that sees perfection when flaws are shown; a love that seeks forever when quitting becomes an option.

If you are questioning what a fear-based relationship looks like, here are just some examples:

- Getting into a relationship because you're lonely

- Giving another the responsibility to make you happy

- Being in a relationship filled with expectations

- Controlling/suppressing/judging/restricting one another

- Overly pleasing the needs of another without giving to yourself

- Giving into the "clock is ticking" mind-set

- Actively engaging in disrespectful language

- Manipulating another for personal gain

- Forcing love

- Being somebody you're not to fit someone else's ideal

DIFFERENCE BETWEEN STANDARDS AND EXPECTATIONS

There is something important we need to address, because some of us might believe that having expectations in a relationship is necessary, or else people could just walk all over us.

Expectations are a fear-based emotion that comes directly from the ego. The ego is what is prideful, and in order for it to protect its pride, it makes expectations on how life should be or how people should behave. I often say that having expectations almost always ends in disappointment because there is no way others are going to uphold the expectations you have of them. Expectations are a form of control and a belief in a limiting world of "giving" with the expectation of "getting," which isn't giving at all.

Giving is a love-based emotion, but when we give for the purpose of receiving, we have tainted this beautiful act with expectation: you are giving for the wrong reasons because expectation comes directly from the ego.

I used to do this quite a bit, not just in my intimate relationships but also with my friends, family members and coworkers. I always believed I was the "giver" in all my relationships. I would always be the go-to for people, where people knew if all else failed, Christal would make it happen. I'm not going to lie: I really liked being "liked" and found my sense of significance in that identity. But there was just one little problem (major problem): I was always pissed when I felt someone didn't reciprocate.

I'd always walk around feeling completely drained because I felt everyone was just so selfish! I'd feel so resentful that I'd often restrict my love from the people I cared about. Expectations turned my gifts against me. To my core, I am a giver, but expecting others to do the same made me feel like I shouldn't be the giver I was. Until I realized that I was the one causing this conflict with my inner self. I had to take a good hard look at why I was giving. Did it come from a place of love, or did it come from a place of fear? That took me all of a split second to figure out because it sure as hell wasn't coming from a place of love if I was frustrated about how people weren't fulfilling my expectations.

Giving, for me, came out of a place of fear. Fear that I wouldn't be good enough if I didn't give. Why, out of all people, would I think so little of myself to believe I wasn't enough already? That's where we get ourselves into a lot of trouble.

We turn our beautiful qualities and gifts into something driven by fear. I see it all the time. There are women who are super successful in their careers but completely unhappy because their drive doesn't come from a place of abundance, but one of fear that they aren't enough. I see women who are dieting on and off because they hate their bodies, rather than having a sustainable healthy lifestyle because they love their bodies.

Expecting things to be different will always cause conflict in our lives, especially because it makes everything personal. Remember what I said about taking things personally? You can't have expectations without taking everything personally, and taking things personally will turn everything into a conflict.

STANDARDS

Now, I don't believe we should be okay with other people taking advantage of us, so here's where the good ol' standards come in.

Standards come from a place of love. Standards are the protectors of our values. They believe we are more than enough to allow less than. When we "value our values," our standards will begin to rise, and when they do, they are in full communication with our truth, or what some like to call our inner guidance system or compass.

Why is this important? Because our inner guide (truth) has a very low tolerance for bullshit. It is what stops us from allowing people into our lives who don't respect the values we live by. It is what stops us from pursuing things that don't expand our souls. When we start raising our standards, our quality of life dramatically increases; we will never have to operate out of fear because our standards come from the love we continuously show ourselves. When there is love flowing internally, there will always be love flowing externally, and without expectations.

The language you speak reflects the relationship you have.

Your relationship will continue to be *"complicated"* if you have to keep making excuses for why you're not being treated right.

You will start to see that the relationships you have will be of quality, that the dreams you pursue will be aligned to your truth and purpose and the activities you engage in will excite and enhance your spirit. Standards are really important to have, and expectations are something we must drop immediately, if we want to become HOT in our relationships.

TOXIC RELATIONSHIPS

Can we talk about a trend I am starting to see in most relationships that's certainly *not* cute?

It's complicated relationships.

Have you ever asked someone about their relationship and they responded, "It's complicated"? For some reason, the more complicated a relationship, the more people want to stay in them! I'm definitely not dismissing myself from this observation, as I've been there and done that, too, but why the hell is this the new standard?

I say, "If it's too complicated to explain, it might be too complicated to sustain." You will continuously say your relationship is complicated if you have to keep making excuses for why you're not being treated right. And there's just no solid reason for why we should settle for relationships that don't make us feel more alive.

Toxic relationships threaten the potential for true passion in life. This isn't just in intimate relationships, either. Toxic relationships happen all across the board. Perhaps it's showing up to a job that completely restricts your spirit and belittles your existence. Or a friendship that is more taking than giving. Or a family member who judges and makes you feel insignificant. Toxic relationships don't just happen in an intimate setting, which often makes them all the more confusing.

If you are in a toxic relationship, the real danger lies with you, because the standards for all relationships begin with you. As we've discussed before, there are many things we might be in a relationship with that are not serving us, but the common denominator for the state of our relationships will always begin with the relationship we have with ourselves first.

Now, even though there are many toxic relationships that we can be a part of, I particularly want to take the time to discuss the signs of a toxic intimate relationship. This is the most asked question I get from women and I feel it is necessary to share.

Toxic intimate relationships that *no one* has time for:

- If you are afraid to leave a relationship for *any* reason, you are in a fear-based relationship.

- If you find yourself feeling jealous and untrusting of your mate, you are in a fear-based relationship.

- If you constantly fight or argue in order to bring passion or even to get attention, you are in a fear-based relationship.

- If you are unable to truly be yourself, you are in a fear-based relationship.

- If you are disrespectful to each other, verbally, emotionally or physically, you are in a fear-based relationship.

- If you do things for your partner hoping for a return, you are in a fear-based relationship.

- If you are afraid of your partner for any reason, you are in a fear-based relationship.

- If you are unable to manage all other areas of your life only to serve your relationship, you are in a fear-based relationship.

- If you try to be the woman your significant other wants you to be and it ultimately conflicts with your truth, you are in a fear-based relationship.

- If you cringe at the thought of communicating your feelings to a significant other, you are in a fear-based relationship.

If you realize that you are in a toxic relationship, by no means is this an easy fix. Toxic relationships around us are a reflection of the toxicity happening within, but it's important to get clear about what is happening and ask the right questions. We can't fix our outer world without shining a light on our inner world.

With that said, here are some questions I'd like you to answer:

- What feeling am I trying to achieve? Example: Is it feeling wanted? Is it not wanting to feel alone?

- What top three emotions do I feel consistently through this relationship? Are there new feelings I'd like to replace these with?

- What two things can I start doing now to connect with myself in positive ways and feel more of how I want to feel without being dependent on the toxic behaviors I'm used to?

A true man will make his woman feel *secure, loved* and *wanted*. A true woman will make her man feel like her *hero*.

Relationships are the most spiritual of practices. They force you to think beyond yourself to the fullest needs of another.

WHAT'S A HEALTHY RELATIONSHIP, ANYWAY?

Dun dun DUNNNN! A beautiful relationship starts with the relationship we have with ourselves and expands outwardly. What does that mean? Well, you've heard me say this before: The relationship we have with ourselves sets the foundation for the relationships we have with others. If we don't know our own worth or value, we couldn't possibly acknowledge or value another, so a beautiful relationship, to me, is one where two people are so filled up with love they have nothing but love to give.

That's not to say there aren't any problems in good relationships, but when we are filled up, we don't have expectations of others to make us feel good—because that just means we put our partners in charge of our happiness. That's a tough job, right? No one should be in charge of our happiness except for us. That is why learning to value yourself and giving yourself permission to be in charge of your own happiness is crucial to building a beautiful relationship with another person. As Don Miguel Ruiz says in his book *The Mastery of Love*, "Happiness never comes from outside of us. He was happy because of the love coming out of him; she was happy because of the love coming out of her."

What does this quote mean? It means we must take happiness into our own hands. It is not your job or responsibility to make your partner happy. It is also not his or her responsibility to make you happy. It is the responsibility of both parties to take ownership of themselves and create a baseline standard for the love they are willing to bring to the relationship. When we each take responsibility for how we show up, we are able to create an abundance of love in our relationships.

There has to be a sense of certainty within yourself before you are able to actually give what is necessary to a relationship. When we come into a partnership feeling insecure of who we are and what we bring to the table, we attract shallow relationships around us—or worse, attract a spouse uncertain of themselves, and insecurity is a dangerous and rocky road.

The other part to this is understanding that we cannot "fix" another person. I know a lot of my ladies out there like to feel needed, and they want to be the person to "fix" their spouses, friends or family members in hopes of making them happier. Putting someone's happiness in your hands is a heavy weight to carry. Could you imagine carrying a dumbbell in your hands for days at a time? How long would it be until you get tired and need to put it down? Pretty quick, right? Being in charge of other people's happiness gets tiring and will prevent you and them from living with purpose and flourishing in the relationship on their own.

Healthy relationships happen to people who understand the importance of how they show up and who find any and all ways to make sure they are taking care of what they need to internally, so that they can be the best partner they can be to their significant other. Does this mean everything will be roses, sunshine and rainbows? Hell no! But here's the thing about taking responsibility for your own emotional state: it allows you both to be more equipped to handle the tough situations together.

Good relationships come from love-based emotions. Healthy relationships come from an abundance of love, and the abundance of love begins with you. Love is the energy we exude from within. This energy is created by feeling good enough and setting the standards that reflect our values. Only then will we be able to fully give to the needs of another.

I often say, "Relationships are the most spiritual of practices. It requires you to think beyond yourself to the fullest needs of another."

Now I know what some of you might be thinking: "Christal, I thought you said we shouldn't give beyond what we have," and you are right. However, giving beyond ourselves to the fullest needs of another is a spiritual practice. It is a practice of contribution and giving, and can only be done once our own spirit is full. When our spirit is full, we attract the relationships that match and reflect what we have to give, which happens to be quite a lot.

A good relationship honors the truth. It honors itself and in turn honors others. A good relationship respects the differences in each other. A good relationship is always growing. A good relationship is two inspired (in-spirit) people who see a grander vision.

CAN YOU FIX A RELATIONSHIP THAT IS STRUGGLING?

As a relationships coach, I 100 percent believe you have the power to transform any relationship. Again, this transformation has nothing to do with the other person and everything to do with you. If you want to fix the connection in any particular relationship in your life, you have to be willing to let go of the expectations you have about the outcome.

You have to understand that you have no control over the other person. You only have control over how you show up and what you understand from the other. You have to be willing to put your ego aside, and that's just not easy. So many times I sit with couples who truly love each other but can't seem to understand each other because of their damn egos. Again, I'm not pointing fingers because I've been there, too, and I still catch myself at times, but the sad thing I've slowly realized is that people like to be right more than they like to love.

Fall in love with someone who DOES the right things, not just SAYS the right things.

As much as you and your partner love each other, if you don't let go of the need to be right and you are constantly playing victim, then your relationship will die. There's no other way of saying it nicely. It may not end, but it will die. It will be harder to trust one another (which we will be discussing in the next chapter). It will be harder to change old patterns. It will be harder to reconnect if you don't let go of the need to prove yourself and show how right you are. Pick your battles or else you will be losing something far more valuable than your ego.

Do you see how these lessons are beginning to connect? Not only do our patterns affect us personally, but they also affect the relationships we have around us.

So, what types of relationships are fixable?

I don't believe all relationships are fixable—such as dangerous, toxic relationships, or ones that are far past disrespecting the sanctity of love. Those I don't believe are fixable. Why? Because when you go down the road of verbally, emotionally and physically abusing each other, you have no respect for yourself and certainly not for the person you are supposed to honor.

Are their different levels of toxicity? Yes, and there's no "one-size-fits-all" approach, but you will know whether a relationship is far past repair. Even if you know the relationship is not fixable, it is still difficult to leave and find a better relationship until you begin to fill your love bucket up by valuing your values and raising your standards.

If you are in a relationship that you know in your heart can be fixed, and it is something you want to put the effort into, my advice to you is this:

- Let go of the expectations you have of this person.

- When you have conversations, check your ego at the door. Only then will you actually hear what needs to be heard.

- Communicate your needs effectively. Ask, what do you both need in the relationship?

- Commit to showing up fully. Make sure the energy you bring around your relationship is full, because only then will love flow.

- Give from a place of love. Stop giving out of fear of not being enough.

Will this solve everything? No, but it will put you in control of how you show up, and that's the only thing you have control over. It will also allow both people to feel like they are being heard. Relationships are all about communication, but a lot of times we expect our significant others (or family or friends) to know how we feel, and that just sets them up for failure. So let go of your expectations, leave your ego at the door, communicate what you need, show up fully every day and give from a place of love. You'll be surprised what this opens up for you, and even if it doesn't save a relationship, your spirit will have grown in this process, making you more mature to handle a good relationship in the future.

Eleven

Plain but
Not So Simple: Trust

"Trust: (n) firm belief in the reliability, truth, ability or strength of someone or something; (v) believe in the reliability, truth, ability or strength of." —Google definition

Before we begin, what does trust mean to you? Not the definition above, but when have you felt that you trusted someone or something? This could be hard for some, but I really want you to think about it. How did you know this was someone you could trust? Or, how did you know it was something you could trust?

Trust is really important in sustaining happiness in our life, but, unfortunately, trust is pretty difficult to feel if we don't understand what it actually means to us. The reason I asked you to recall the last time you felt you could trust someone is so you can pick out what your rules are for trusting another person.

Trust is different for everyone. It is something that is achieved or felt for different reasons. There is no right or wrong, but if we can dissect this, like most of the feelings we've examined throughout this book, then we can really get clear on how we can trust in grander schemes.

What do I mean? I mean trusting that life is working in our favor, even when it doesn't feel like it. But how can we trust in life if it's hard for us to trust in people? Relationships are all about trust, but a lack of trust is what damages the potential for most relationships, especially for those of us who've been hurt in the past.

Can I vent to you a little? I have a problem with one of the definitions listed above regarding trust: "firm belief in the reliability, truth, ability or strength of someone or something." That is how most of us would define trust, right? But there's actually a problem with that.

Having a firm belief is like having expectations of how something should be, and remember what I said about expectations? Now, we can argue that this isn't necessarily what this definition is implying, but I do realize—without knowing the actual meaning of *trust*—that we are coming up with some solid black-and-white rules for how we should feel trust. These rules are almost certainly keeping us feeling uncertain in ourselves, in others and in life.

Trust is all about vulnerability, and to be vulnerable requires us to be open to what could go wrong.

What?! Yes.

That's the exact reason why we can't trust to begin with, right? Because we fear all the things that can go wrong from opening ourselves up to vulnerability. I told you this trust thing isn't easy, but what you have to remember is there is no fulfillment in life without trust.

Let me repeat that again … There is no fulfillment in life if you aren't able to trust in it. To trust in life means to trust in ourselves. That is where true certainty comes in. Sounds like quite the contradiction, right? Certainty and trust: certainty is knowing, and trust is taking a chance. How do they coexist?

Like yin and yang, vulnerability and certainty are intertwined in a beautiful and balanced world. In order to be vulnerable, you have to know you are safe (certainty). And to truly feel safe, you have to put yourself out there—be vulnerable—in order to know. That's how trust is built.

When I look back at the times I've built trust with people in my life, that trust was almost always built on times I was most vulnerable and scared. Relationships get stronger with the constant flow between vulnerability and certainty. The more vulnerable, the more certain you are about your safety in being vulnerable, but you wouldn't be able to know that without trusting first.

Remember I told you about the conversation I had with my girlfriend in the kitchen when I didn't know what was causing me anxiety? Opening up and being vulnerable allowed me to truly see the depth of our relationship and just how much I could trust her, and I was able to grow a stronger connection with her.

No relationship would be sustainable without trust. Absolutely no relationship. It doesn't matter whether it's a business relationship, a friendship, intimate or otherwise: trust is absolutely crucial and grows over time. But here's the thing: trust, like love, is felt differently by everyone. There is no one-size-fits-all. If I were to take ten people into a room, we all may have the same general theories of trust, but if we all were to get very specific on how we feel it most, your answer would be different from mine.

The less you try to shape things, the more they *fall in your favor.*

Even the trust between Andrew and me is completely different. Sure, we have the same deal breakers, but the way he feels trust in a relationship comes from factors way different than mine.

In *The Five Love Languages*, author Gary Chapman discusses how each person speaks his or her own love language and it is our duty to understand how our partners speak. Based on their love language, they receive love differently from how we may receive it. I'm starting to believe it is the same with trust. The way we like to receive love could be reflective of the way we slowly build trust.

I strongly encourage you to read *The Five Love Languages*, but just to give you a little insight on what I'm talking about, here are the five languages:

- Acts of service

- Quality time

- Words of affirmation

- Physical touch

- Receiving gifts

I am a "quality time" and "acts of service" type of gal, while Andrew is "physical touch" (I'm sure a lot of men are, ha-ha). Knowing this, I've been able to tie together our similarities so that we can each feel loved. And love is just a feeling interlaced with trust, isn't it?

Let me ask you, could you be in love with someone but not trust them? I can already hear the responses: "Christal, of course you can be in love with someone and not trust them. That was the problem with my past relationship." This is exactly what we need to discuss.

LOVE AND TRUST

Let's take love out of the equation for a moment, because love can still be a little confusing when it has to do with relationships. Why? Because even the most toxic relationships feel love but may not feel trust. So we are going to break it down to simply "liking" someone.

Can you like a person you don't trust? Think of your closest friendships: What makes those relationships so close? They are close because you "like" those people for who they are and "like" how you feel around them, right? Let's dissect it a bit further. Would you feel good around them if you didn't trust them? Probably not.

Think of that one person who makes you feel good about being you. You feel good about yourself around him or her because you are able to be authentic, expressive and vulnerable, and that takes *trust*.

Can you have a relationship without trust? Yes, you can. Will it be sustainable? No, it will not. Why? Because trust allows a certain part of your truth to be expressed, and your truth can't be expressed without trust that someone is going to provide you with some safety.

Intimate relationships need more "liking" instead of "loving." What? Yes, even as a relationship coach, I think liking the person you are with creates a more stable and sustainable relationship. It's just not enough to love someone without feeling good while you're around him or her.

I see so many individuals in intimate relationships seek refuge in other people because they feel like they can be more of who they are around others than around their significant other. Why? Because they don't feel like they can trust their significant other with who they are. When you trust someone so intimately, you tend to like being around him or her, and if you don't "like" the person you are with, it will be pretty hard to sustain that relationship.

Sure, love is important, and I'm not discounting love, but I believe in simplifying our relationships. I find that the people in relationships who actually "like" being around each other have more trust than those who say they love each other but don't "like" each other.

CAN YOU HAVE A RELATIONSHIP WITHOUT TRUST?

You certainly can have a relationship without trust, but will it be sustainable? Probably not. Trust is necessary to create a united vision. In order for an intimate relationship to thrive, there needs to be a collaboration that comes from understanding, which comes from openness, which comes from trust.

As a woman, I need to trust the people closest to me in order for me to feel free. If I don't feel free around the people I care about, then how can I possibly bring positive energy around us? If I don't trust someone, I feel restricted and uncertain of not only myself but the other person as well, and there is no way a healthy relationship can thrive in that type of environment.

Intimately, a woman needs to feel safe. The feminine energy needs to feel as if she can be expressive, and for that to happen she needs to feel trust. If I didn't trust my man it would most certainly shut down our intimate life, because for me to even open up sexually I need to feel safe enough to do so. A lack of trust will just make two people insecure. When we don't feel safe, there is nothing we can grow upon in a relationship. Let's take a skyscraper, for instance. Before a building is built, there are geotechnical engineers who test the rocks and soil of the ground to evaluate its stability before the site is ready for construction.

Sometimes *liking* the person you are with is more important than *loving* them. Anyone can misinterpret the meaning of love, but when you like being around the person you are with, well that's just powerful!

I think of a relationship in the same terms. Trust is like the base of a relationship, just as the ground is the base of any building. In order for a skyscraper to be built, the ground must be stable enough for it. Same goes with any relationship. In order to consistently build and grow a relationship, there needs to be a solid foundation. Trust is at the base of any relationship because from there, it can handle the weight of life, and let's be real—intimate relationships need all the stability they can get.

Not having trust in the relationship is like building a tall building and realizing midway through construction that it will not be able to stand the tests of Mother Nature. I see lack of trust the same way. As soon as you bring in an element of life (stressors), it will more than likely crumble.

Nothing can be built on a rocky foundation, yet I see many relationships believing it can. I definitely thought that way in past relationships. I used to think the opposite about trust. I believed that major life experiences would build trust in the relationship, and to a certain degree, that can be true. However, I quickly realized that without trust, my relationship was toxic from the start, because I wouldn't believe anything my ex-boyfriend said. Instead of my intimate relationship being a relief from life's problems, it was the biggest problem in my life.

I found myself uneasy, unhappy and completely disconnected from my truth, all because there was no solid foundation of trust. I couldn't open myself as a woman without knowing I was safe, and lord knows I was not emotionally safe with him.

I'm in disbelief every time I hear a lady say, "I have a really good relationship, I just don't really trust my man."

How can you have a really good relationship if you don't trust the person you are with? This is when we need to take on the first lesson discussed in the beginning of this book, which is to "Get real!" Sorry not sorry for the tough love. We need to understand the contradictions in the things we say. Getting real addresses the problem head-on without sugarcoating it with a "but it's good."

CAN YOU REBUILD DAMAGED TRUST?

This is where trust gets "not so simple." Do I believe you can rebuild trust? Absolutely! But this is entirely up to each individual depending upon the amount of pain the "betrayal" caused them. If a relationship started on a firm foundation of trust and somewhere down the line trust was compromised, then I do believe there are ways to build trust in the relationship again, if both parties do the work.

What does that mean? That means regardless of who broke the trust to begin with, both parties are required to work together to rebuild it. I often see people punishing their spouses for a betrayal of trust when in fact, that also damages trust. What did we discuss before? We talked about letting go of the need to victimize yourself or to be right. The more we do that, the harder it is to trust your spouse again because you will continue living in the past of what happened. No matter what, if you decide to stay in a relationship after a breakdown of trust, then it is also your responsibility to be a part of the rebuilding of your relationship.

Although one person might be seen as the betrayer of trust, usually there were tiny breaks of trust along the way from both parties, until one of them committed a huge act. But you will never see your involvement in it if you see yourself as a victim.

Again, I believe trust can be rebuilt if the relationship had a strong foundation of trust to begin with. I don't think relationships that have a wobbly foundation to begin with can be rebuilt because there's really nothing to rebuild.

Now, to flip the script, you can even rebuild trust with a family member you thought wronged you. Take my mom, for example. Once I got over playing victim, I was able to allow my mom to show up as the new woman she is, and every time I got out of her way, she was able to show me she was trustworthy. But it wasn't just her "proving" herself to me; it was also me doing my part to restore trust with her. My mother and I are beyond close now, and I know she would be there at the drop of a hat, so I'm thankful to have rebuilt our relationship.

Do we have to rebuild trust with people? No. But you also can't have a flourishing relationship without it. Not every relationship should be worked on, and it is up to you to choose the ones worth rebuilding. However, should you choose to rebuild trust in a relationship, you have to participate. If you're thinking someone owes you, then you are not building trust, you are pointing the finger, and I don't know about you, but I just couldn't trust someone who pointed their finger at me.

TRUST OFFERS NO CERTAINTIES

Oh boy! This is hard because as much as I talk about how trust provides safety in a relationship, it's also not certain … eek! I know, this is what usually fucks people up because we like to know everything and we aren't fans of surprises especially ones that could potentially hurt us, but this is something we have to understand. Trust is faith.

Let me say this again: Trust is faith!

When you believe in yourself, you attract more people who *believe in you, too.*

You may think that faith is usually tied to a religion, but it's not. Coming from someone who's not religious but very spiritual, I believe faith is the ability to give in to the unknown. We don't know everything that's going to happen and we don't need to, but trying to protect ourselves from pain takes away from all the beauty life has to offer.

Trust goes beyond just relationships. It is walking around every day knowing that life is happening for us. The more we give up the need to control every aspect of our lives, the more we will be able to see the miracles happening around us. We just have to trust that they will. Bad experiences, troubled relationships and the pitfalls of life are all part of the journey, but we won't see that if we can't trust.

You can't have fulfilling relationships without trust. You can't feel happiness without trust. You can't live with purpose if you can't trust. Life is about making the most out of what you can see instead of protecting yourself from what you can't see.

Will people hurt us? Yes.

Will you fall down and scrape your knees? Yes.

Will you get lost? Yes.

Will things not work out for you at times? Yes.

But you will also have people that will love you unconditionally.

You will have people who will help you back up if you fall.

You will have guidance when you are lost.

You will have tons of things that work in your favor.

You just have to choose to see it that way, and trust that you have all you need within to make the best decisions going forward. Trust that you know how to attract the best relationships around you. Trust that you are exactly where you need to be in your journey to accept the lessons of today and to do the very best you can with those lessons. Trust that you are worthy of love and are more than good enough. Trust that you have more than enough love and energy to give.

Now strut how HOT you are on the streets and to the world. Being HOT is absolutely necessary for us to live out our purpose, and now you know what that takes.

Before you walk your HOT ass out to the world, though, there is one last practice I'd like you to do, and I will do it with you!

The Practice: How to Be HOT

1. Sit in a quiet space alone.

2. You may play peaceful music to truly get yourself in the zone.

3. Ask yourself for forgiveness. For example, "[Insert your name], please forgive me for not living in a truly connected space with you. I know you've been trying to talk to me and I have not listened or trusted in you."

4. Make a powerful statement, such as, "Starting today I will listen to your guidance and stop listening to fear. I know fear is not the core of who I am; YOU are my core, my spirit, my truth, and with your guidance I know I will make a life full of trust, love and abundance. I give you my word, and above that, my actions!"

5. Say who you are and what you stand for. For example, "I will be a woman of love, dignity, compassion and influence!" (You can make up your own.) Repeat this five times.

6. Express what these new actions will give to your life. For example, "Living truthfully will allow me to live my life fearlessly, giving selflessly to the people I love and creating more powerful and deeper relationships."

7. Most importantly, don't judge or criticize yourself for being "corny." This is a nonjudgmental space. It is a time to truly connect to the person who is buried inside. Create an environment of peace and freedom.

8. Now, move to the music you have on and dance! Don't be shy: DANCE! Moooove that HOT, sexy body of yours and be a woman of influence, love and power!

When you walk out into the world I want you to remember that being HOT is an attitude. An attitude fueled by love, not fear. Love is what fuels all the beauty in our lives, and you are worthy of every bit of love this world has to offer.

With that said, in order for us to live in a space that is happy, open and trusting, we have to remove ourselves from the attachments we have to what has happened, what others have done to us and the mistakes we've made in the past.

Who you are is bigger than any stage of life you will go through.

Always remember that.

You have every bit of what is necessary within you now to make your life what you want it to be. The only thing standing in your way is you. Beliefs can limit or empower us, and our job is to reconstruct the beliefs we have about life and love to something that makes us believe in our greatest potential.

So, I ask you now, how were you standing in the way of your own happiness? And, how are you committed to showing up for yourself now?

Like I said before, the best attention you will ever receive is the attention you give yourself. Start showing up for yourself, my darling, because the rest of the relationships in your life depend on it.

And always stay HOT!

Acknowledgments

There are so many people who have played a significant role in my life. Without a doubt, I wouldn't be doing what I do or be the person I am today without them.

So let me start with the ladies of my life. (Duh! Ladies first.)

To my mom, Linette: It is safe to say I wouldn't be doing what I do if I hadn't had the struggles we went through in our early life. Your heart is so big and filled with so much love, and I am so lucky to have the support I have from you. Thank you for always being there and being my biggest spiritual teacher and best friend. I love you so much and am so honored to be your daughter.

To my sister, Lashante: You are my love. I can't thank the universe enough for making me your sister. You are the strongest girl I know, and you have so much to give. Thank you for always being there for me.

To my stepmom, Coco: Thank you for coming into my life at a young age and treating me with all the love a young girl would ever need. There has never been a time you couldn't be there for me. Thank you for also showing me what a beautiful relationship looks like. You and my dad are perfection.

To my mother-"un"-law, Anita: I couldn't be any more blessed to have such a beautiful extension to my family. Thank you for bringing Andrew into the world and for giving me all the love a daughter-un-law could ever need. I love you to the moon!

To my grandma, Connie: You are who I want to be when I grow up. You are my best friend and inspiration. Thank you for always being there for me and inspiring me through your constant devotion to our family. Words can't even describe how much you mean to me. Spirit animal! Idol! #womancrusheveryday.

To my grandma, Louise: You are Wonder Woman! There is no one who can do it all like you. Thank you for all you have done for my sister and me and for showing unconditional love throughout our trials and tribulations. Above all, you are the funniest woman I know!

To my Aunt Rosie and my best friend, Pamela: You two keep me on my toes. Thank you for your unconditional love and support. I have laughed, cried and shared my dreams with you both and I couldn't have asked for a better support system!

Now for the beautiful men in my life:

To my dad, Charles: Thank you, thank you, thank you for being the best dad a girl could ever have, seriously. Because of you, I felt so loved even when I was at my lowest. You are my hero. Thank you for always putting your needs second to give me what I needed. I love you so much!

To my grandpa, Hollis: I will always cherish our walks around the golf course. I will always cherish our long talks on the porch. If I could be like anyone on this planet, you'd be one of them. I don't know how I'd have turned out if I hadn't had the love and wisdom you always gave me and my sister growing up. Thank you for being our hero!

To my grandpa, Cocoy: Thank you for making my grandma Louise so happy! You are such a patient and loving man with an accent I will never get sick of hearing. I love you so much!

To my grandpa, Hector: Even though you are gone, I will never get over you. You were my very first best friend and love. You were also my first heartache. I think about you every day since you've been gone and couldn't go without saying thank you, as I do believe you still guide me to this very day. I am thankful for the time I was able to have with you because it shaped me hugely! Love you more than words could say.

And for those outside the family:

To Maureen and Joe Mckenna, my mentors. There's no couple I admire more than you both. Thank you for always being there for me even when you didn't have to. Thank you for showing me what fifty-one years of marriage looks like. Thank you for giving me all the tools, resources and inspiration to do what I needed to in life and business. I love you both so much and am so thankful to have you both as an extension of my family. P.S. Thank you, Joe, for guiding me to doing what I am doing now.

To Erin Simone: I am so blessed to have a friend like you. You are a person I can trust telling anything to. You have a way of really showing up. Thank you for all you are in my life and for being a HUGE supporter of my journey.

To team TLC, Alex and Chrissy: I am so thankful to have you both come in and work every day to make my dream a reality! Blessed!

A big fat thank-you to Page Street Publishing for believing in me enough to write my first book. I pinch myself every day that you all approached me. Thank you for helping me get my message out to the world. You all are amazing!

Thank you to the ladies I've met throughout my TLC journey who have supported me tremendously along the way. You all are so selfless and generous. Thank you for being my cheerleaders and spreading my message in every way you can to the world. I love you so much! (You know who you are!)

About the Author

Christal Fuentes is the founder of The Ladies Coach. She lives and breathes her belief that you can't find fulfillment in life without mastering the art of relationships. She aims to provide women with a digital platform to enhance their life and relationships through free tools and resources at TheLadiesCoach.com.

Let's connect!

Website: theladiescoach.com

Facebook: www.facebook.com/TheLadiesCoach/?fref=ts

Instagram/Twitter: @theladiescoach

Snapchat: @christalfuentes

Did you have an "aha" moment? Let Christal know by using the hashtag: #How2bHot.

Index

N

needs

acknowledging your own, 47–48

"six human," list of, 82

to be right, 35–36, 38–43, 45

negative energy, taking responsibility for, 92, 95

"no," saying, 47–55

not taking it personally, 57–58, 61–65

O

openness

and confusion, 26

and finding your passion, 105–6, 109–112, 115–17

P

pain and fear, quote about, 61

passion, finding, 105–6, 109–112, 115–17

playful, being, and happiness, 82

pleasing people, 26, 47–48, 103

pleasures versus habits, 54

"Power of Vulnerability, The" (TED talk) (Brown), 72

practices

compassion, 64–65

Ho'o Pono Pono ("to make right") prayer, 42–43

how to be HOT, 147

saying "no," 55

"turn it on," for exploring, 111–112

values, list of, 30–31

prayer, Ho'o Pono Pono, 42–43

present, being, and happiness, 87

putting yourself down, 102

Q

quotes

by Alicia Keys, 114

by Amy Schumer, 81

about attention, 29

about "baggage," 75

about changing yourself, 53

by Danielle LaPorte, 108

about fooling yourself, 18

about finding bad versus good, 70

about hardship, 37

about insecurities, 94

by Jill Bolte Taylor, 92

by Lala Anthony, 33

about laughter, 86

about listening to